ADDITIONS AND CORRECTIONS

TO THE

W.P.A.

INVENTORY

OF

TRUMBULL COUNTY, OHIO:

WARREN

Jana Sloan Broglin

HERITAGE BOOKS
2025

HERITAGE BOOKS

AN IMPRINT OF HERITAGE BOOKS, INC.

Books, CDs, and more—Worldwide

For our listing of thousands of titles see our website
at
www.HeritageBooks.com

Published 2025 by
HERITAGE BOOKS, INC.
Publishing Division
5810 Ruatan Street
Berwyn Heights, MD 20740

(Originally Titled)
INVENTORY OF THE COUNTY ARCHIVES OF OHIO
Prepared by
Historical Records Survey
Division of Women's and Professional Projects
Works Progress Administration

No. 78. TUMBULL COUNTY (WARREN)

Columbus, Ohio
Historical Records Survey
April 1937

International Standard Book Number
Paperbound: 978-0-7884-5050-1

County Offices and Their Records

TABLE OF CONTENTS

2nd edition

In 1929 after the stock market crash along with the Great Depression, the drought of 1930, and crop failures which followed, President Herbert Hoover and his successor Franklin D. Roosevelt formulated relief projects, the most successful was the establishment of the Works Progress Administration (WPA).

Established as the Works Projects Administration in 1935, the WPA was the largest of the many programs developed during Roosevelt's "New Deal." In 1939, the agency's name was changed to Works Progress Administration, and continued as such until its demise in 1943.

The Federal Writers' Project, a division of the WPA (known as Federal Project Number One), created jobs for many unemployed librarians, clerks, researchers, editors, and historians. The workers went to courthouses, town halls, offices in large cities, vital statistics offices and inventoried records. Besides indexing works, many records were transcribed. One of these many projects was the *Inventory of the County Archives* which has benefitted genealogists and historians. The inventories listed the records, either by volumes or file boxes and years per record type, within the office. Although the WPA oversaw this project, the information for each volume of records may differ significantly by the information submitted.

Many of these volumes included in the *Inventory of the County Archives* contain listings of records initiated specifically for the depression era. Records may include volumes for the WPA, CCC (Civilian Conservation Corps), as well as for tuberculosis hospitals. These listings may include the names of the workers.

The information herein is verbatim using the vernacular of the time. Obvious spelling errors have been corrected. Records listed may have met the requirement for retention and have been destroyed as per the records retention act, while other records are considered permanent records. Records once considered "open" to the public, such as lunacy, idiotic, and juvenile cases, or records involving children, such as children's homes, and school records may be "closed" due to a revision of state laws. (*See:* **https://codes.ohio.gov/ohio-revised-code** Ohio Revised Code, sections 149.31 and 149.34). However, the records may be opened to family members with adequate proof of lineage.

PREFACE
2nd edition

Although this project was to encompass all of Ohio's 88 counties, approximately 30 of these inventories have been located while others may not have been done, lost, or are located in libraries and not known to the general public.

Volumes follow a general format listing the offices. Those for Fulton, Medina, Muskingum, and Wayne include either additional information or may be lacking segments found in other volumes as these were "missing" books.

The addresses and website section of this edition lists an up-to-date location guide to each office mentioned. Non-governmental websites may list locations where documentation for the county may be found.

Jana Sloan Broglin
Fellow, Ohio Genealogical Society
Swanton, Ohio
2025

The Survey of State and Local Historical Records was initiated as a nation-wide undertaking in January 1936, as a part of the Federal Writers' Project of the Works Progress Administration. In Ohio the Survey began operations in February 1936, under the administrative supervision of James G. Dunton, State Director of the Writers' Project, and under the technical supervision of Dr. William D. Overman, State Archivist and Curator of History, Ohio State Archaeological and Historical Society. In sixteen districts of the Works Progress Administration in Ohio, the project was organized and operated by the district supervisors of the Writers' Project. In November 1936, the Survey became an independent part of Federal Project No. 1, but its administration and operation in Ohio remained unchanged.

The objective of the Survey in Ohio has been the preparation of complete inventories of the records of the State and of each county, city, and other local governmental units. Although a condensed form of entry is used, information is given as to the limiting dates of all extant records, the contents of individual series, and the location of records in state house, county courthouse, or other depository. The record titles are arranged under office of origin and by subject; in the index they are arranged alphabetically but with cross references. Preceding the record entries for each office is a brief statement as to the history, functions, and records of the office.

The *Inventory of County Archives in Ohio* will, when completed, consist of a separate number for each county in the state. The units of the series are numbered according to the respective position of the county in an alphabetical list of the counties. Thus, the inventory herewith presented for Trumbull County is No. 78. The inventory of the state archives and of municipal and other local records will constitute separate publications.

The survey in Trumbull County was started February 16, 1936, and was completed in June of that year under the direction of H. O. Allison, district supervisor. During the progress of the survey it was a common occurrence for county officials to request information from our workers concerning the location of certain records. Genuine co-operation was received from all county officials. Many of them expressed their personal approval of the survey. For the completeness and accuracy of the inventory, the project personnel in Trumbull County has been entirely responsible; the state office staff, under Dr. Overman and John O. Marsh, editorial supervisor, contributed the legal histories and did the final editing.

Preface
1st edition

The various units of the *Inventory of County Archives* will be issued in mimeographed form for free distribution to State and local public officials and public libraries in Ohio, and to a limited number of libraries and government agencies outside the State. Requests for information concerning particular units of the Inventory should be addressed to Dr. William D. Overman, Ohio State Museum, Columbus, Ohio.

The Historical Records Survey in Ohio is part of the nation-wide project which bears the same name. General regulations and procedures applicable to all project units in the 48 states have been followed in Ohio. It would be ungracious of me not to point out, however, that credit for the unusually high standard of administrative and editorial work achieved by the survey in Ohio should be given entirely to Mr. Dunton, Dr. Overman, their staff and workers, and the officials of WPA in Ohio who have always given the project such cordial support and assistance. I also desire to express my appreciation for the unfailing interest and cooperation of Trumbull County officials in our undertaking.

Luther H. Evans
National Supervisor
Historical Records Survey
Washington, D. C.

April 2, 1937

adm. . . . . administration
am. . . . . amended
Arch. . . . . Archaeological
Art. . . . . Article
bull. . . . . bulletin
c. . . . . copyright
capias . . . . a warrant or order for arrest of a person,
typically issued by the judge or magistrate in a case.
CCC. . . . . Civilian Conservation Corps
certiorari. . . . . to be more fully informed
chap (s). . . . . chapter(s)
comp. . . . . compiler
Const. . . . . Constitution
ed(s). . . . . editor(s)
et al. . . . . (et alii), and others
(et) passim . . . . and here and there
ex officio . . . . as a result of one's status or position
et seq. . . . . and following
fee simple . . . . full and irrevocable ownership
G. C. . . . . General Code
habeas corpus . . . . protection against illegal imprisonment
ibid. . . . . the same reference
LL.D. . . . . Doctor of Laws
loc. cit. . . . . *(coco citato)*
N.P. . . . . The Ohio NISI PRIUS REPORTS
n. p. . . . . no place of publication shown
n. s. . . . . new series
nolle prosequi . . . . notice of abandonment by a
plaintiff or prosecutor of all or part of a suit or action
O.L. . . . . *Laws of Ohio*
op. cit. . . . . *(opere citato)* In the work cited
posse comitatus . . . . a group of citizens called upon to assist the sheriff
praecipe . . . . a written request for action
prima facie . . . . on the first impression
pro rata . . . . in proportion

procedendo . . . . sends case from appellate court to a lower court
pt. . . . . part
quo warranto. . . . . by what authority or warrant
replevins . . . . return of personal property
wrongfully taken or held by a defendant
R. . . . . River
rep. . . . . reporter
R.S. . . . . Revised Statutes
sec(s). . . . . section(s)
sic . . . . thus, following copy
supersedeas . . . . a stay of enforcement of a judgment pending appeal
v. . . . . versus
venires . . . . a group of people summoned for jury duty
vol(s). . . . . volume(s)
WPA . . . . Works Progress/Projects Administration
writ . . . . a formal, legal document, a decree
x . . . . by
— . . . . current, to date
4-H . . . . (Four - H)

Each chapter or section of "County Offices and Their Records" consists of an essay describing the legal status and functions of one department of county government and an inventory of the records of that department.

Each record constitutes a separate entry. Entries are arranged under topical headings and subheadings.

Each entry sets forth, insofar as applicable, the following:

1. Entry number. Entries are numbered consecutively throughout the inventory.
2. The exact title as it appears on the record, or if the record has no title a supplied title in brackets. If the title of the record is non-descriptive, misleading, or incorrect, an additional title (in capitals and lowercase letters), also enclosed in brackets, has been supplied.
3. Dates show inclusive years or parts of years covered by the record. Breaks in dates indicate that the record is missing or was not kept between dates shown. A dash in place of the final date indicates an open record. If no current entries have been made the date of the last entry is noted. Where no statement is made that the record was discontinued at the last date shown, it could not be definitely established that such was the case. Where no comment is made on the absence of prior and subsequent records, no definite information could be obtained.
4. Quantity, given in chronological order wherever possible.
5. Labeling. Numbers and letters within parentheses indicate labeling on volumes, file boxes, or other containers.
6. Variations in title. The current or most recent title is used but significant variations are shown with dates for which each was used.
7. Change of agency. Occasionally a record is discontinued as a county record and kept by some other agency.
8. Description. A statement of the nature and purpose of the record and of what the record shows. As the contents of a record may vary, over time the description may differ somewhat from the record at any one period. Wherever feasible, changes in content are shown with dates. In map and plat entries the names of author and publisher and the scale are omitted only when not available.

9. Arrangement. Records said to be alphabetically arranged are frequently alphabetized only as to initial letter of the surname. This is true especially where there is a secondary arrangement.

10. Indexing. Self-contained indexes are described in the entry. Separate indexes constitute separate entries with cross references to and from the record entry.

11. Nature of recording. Changes are indicated with dates.

12. Condition. No statement is made if good or excellent.

13. Number of pages. Averaged for the series.

14. Dimensions show size of volumes, maps, file boxes, or other containers and are expressed in inches in every instance. The dimensions of volumes are given in order of height, width, and thickness; of file boxes in order of height, width, and depth.

15. Location. Rooms referred to are in the county courthouse unless some other building is specified.

Title line cross references are used to complete series where a record is kept separately for a period of time or in other records for different periods of time. They are also used in all artificial entries which are made to show, under their proper office, records kept in the same volume or files with records of another office. In both instances, the description of the master entry shows the title and entry number of the record from which the cross reference is made. Dates shown in the description of the master entry are for the part or parts of the record contained therein, and are shown only when they vary from those of the master entry. Artificial entries show only title, dates, and description.

Separate third paragraph cross references from entry to entry, are used to show prior, subsequent, or related records which are not a part of the same series. If, however, both entries are under the same subject headings, no third paragraph references are made. "See also" references from subject headings refer to entries in the same department which contain records logically belonging under that heading but which have been classified under an equally appropriate heading.

Trumbull County, Ohio, with an area of 633 square miles is located in the northeastern part of the state. Warren, a city of 41,062 population, is the county seat. The area within the present territorial limits of the county, like that of other counties in the state, was at one time claimed by France who rested her claims on the discoveries of Cartier and the subsequent explorations of LaSalle and Marquette. England, the rival of the French for possession of the territory west of the Alleghenies, based her claim on the discoveries of Cabot, the sea-to-sea charters granted to the original colonies, and upon the priority of occupation of the seacoast. (Reuben Gold Thwaites, *France in America, 1497-1763.* Amer. Nation Ser. VII, 43, 89-104). France resisted the claims of England and defended the territory by force of arms until 1763, when, by the Treaty of Paris, the entire territory was ceded to England. (Thwaites, *op. cit.,* 143ff).

The sea-to-sea charters granted to the English colonies were to complicate the formation of a confederation following American Independence. Connecticut, as well as Virginia, North Carolina, and Georgia, claimed lands between the Alleghenies and the Mississippi in accordance with the original grants. In ceding her claims Connecticut, wishing to foster religion and education in the state, reserved certain lands in northern Ohio for the use of her own citizens. This land, lying between the forty-ninth parallel and the northern boundary of the United States, extended one hundred and twenty miles west of the Pennsylvania line. (Andrew Cunningham McLaughlin, *The Confederation and the Constitution 1783-1789* Amer. Nation. Ser., X, 112). This territory became known as the Connecticut Western Reserve or the Western Reserve. In 1792 the Connecticut Legislature gave a half million acres of land comprising the western half of the Reserve to the inhabitants of New London and other towns of the state whose property had been burned by the British during the American Revolution. (B. A. Hinsdale, *The Old Northwest*, New York, 1888, 369-370. The publications of the Firelands Historical Society contain many documents and articles relating to the Reserve).

Due to the difficulties of transportation, as well as the hostility of the Indians along the routes of travel from the seaboard states to the west, Connecticut found it impossible to attract individual buyers. Accordingly she sold the entire tract, save the Firelands, to a group of land speculators who styled themselves the Connecticut Land Company. (Beverly Bond, *The Civilization of the Old Northwest.* New York, 1934, 25-26. For an interesting discussion of rival speculating companies in the Reserve, see Claud L. Shepard, "The Connecticut Land Company: A Study of the Beginnings of Colonization of the Western Reserve," in *Western*

Reserve Historical Society Tracts, no. 96, 69-96). Moses Cleaveland, one of the agents of the company, led a group of surveyors into the territory in 1796. He quieted the claims of the Iroquois to the lands east of the Cuyahoga River by giving them a cash payment, "2 Beef Cattle & 100 gall of Whisky." (Elbert Jay Benton, Ed., *Journal of Seth Pease to and from New Connecticut, 1796-98, Western Reserve Historical Society Tract,* no. 94, pt. ii, 38-39). Surveys were begun at once at the mouth of the Cuyahoga River. In surveying the tract a five-mile township was established instead of a six-mile area as used by congress. By 1801 there were 1,303 residents in the Reserve. (Clarence Edwin Carter. *The Territorial Papers of the United States.* III, 199).

Neither the federal government nor the state of Connecticut attempted to organize local government administration until 1800. The purchasers of lands held their titles under the laws of Connecticut; they could not submit to the government established under the Ordinance of 1787 without endangering their land titles. On the other hand, the civil jurisdiction of Connecticut could not be extended over them without much inconvenience. The land holders, wishing to have a stable government in the territory, appealed to the Connecticut Legislature to cede civil jurisdictions of the territory to the United States. (*American State Papers, Public Lands,* I, 98). Accordingly, in October 1797, the state of Connecticut ceded its political rights in the territory to the United States. (*U. S. Statutes at Large,* III, 57; Salmon P. Chase, ed., *The Statutes of Ohio and of the Northwest Territory,* 2 volumes, Cincinnati, 1833, 64-66).

St. Clair, governor-general of the Northwest Territory, was directed by the secretary of state to erect the Western Reserve into a county. The governor, on July 10, 1800, issued a proclamation creating Trumbull County which included the entire Western Reserve. Warren, established in 1800 by Ephraim Quimby, a member of the Connecticut Land Company, was made the county seat. (Clarence Edwin Carter, *The Territorial Papers of the United States,* III, 525). The governor-general commissioned David Abbott, sheriff; John Stark, recorder; Calvin Pease, prothonotary of the court of common pleas; and John Levitt, probate judge. A general commission was issued for the court of quarter session and for the court of common pleas which directed the courts to meet quarterly at the county seat. (Carter, *op. cit.,* III, 525).

The first courtroom was a bower of trees "standing between two corn cribs." The seat of justice consisted of a dozen log cabins. The court of quarter session appointed a committee to divide the county into townships. The committee established eight townships known as Youngstown, Warren, Hudson, Vernon, Richland, Painesville, Middlefield, and Cleveland. (H. Z. Williams & Son, ed., *History of Trumbull and Mahoning Counties*. 2 volumes, Cleveland, 1882, I, 68-71). On September 22, 1800 the governor-general issued writs of elections to the sheriff which directed him to hold elections for representatives as provided by law. (Carter, *op. cit.,* 525).

Ohio entered the Union in 1803. The sheriff, coroner, and commissioners, which, during the territorial period, had been appointed officials now became elective ones. In 1805 Trumbull County was divided by the creation of Geauga County. (4 O. L. 65). With the creation of Ashtabula and Portage Counties in 1807, Trumbull County took practically its present boundaries. (6 O. L. 3).

The first county courthouse was built in 1815. Previous to this time various cabins had housed the courts, county officials, and their records. A county jail was completed in 1824. By 1840 the first courthouse being then in bad repair and inadequate, enterprising citizens, realizing the value of the public records, circulated a petition asking for the construction of a new building. But the discussion gave rise to an extensive dispute between Warren and Youngstown as to the permanent location of the county seat. The citizens of Youngstown, unwilling to contribute to the further advancement of Warren, demanded a division of Trumbull County and the erection of a new county with Youngstown as the county seat. Canfield complicated matters by petitioning the legislature for the erection of an additional county out of the 10 southern townships of Trumbull County and the five northern townships of Columbiana County. The last proposition received the approval of the legislature in 1846 and a new county designated as Mahoning County with Canfield and later (1876) Youngstown as the county seat. (44 O. L. 116-117).

Thus relieved from the opposition of Youngstown, the citizens of Warren continued their agitation for a new county building. The Trumbull County courthouse was begun in 1852 and completed in 1854. (*Western Reserve Democrat*, March 29, 1895). This courthouse was practically destroyed by fire in 1895 (*Ibid.*). The present courthouse was begun in 1895 and was ready for occupancy two years later. (*Ibid.,* April 2, 5, 8, 16, 1897).

Trumbull County, like other counties in the Reserve, was settled largely by Connecticut people. The settlers brought with them the usual New England support of education and religion. But in the newer west, where frontier democracy taught the political and social equality of man, the influence of the Calvinistic rigidity of the church was somewhat softened. Albeit the social, cultural, and religious heritage derived from New England continued to color the lives of the people for generations. (Hinsdale, *op. cit.*, 388-392). The population increased from 15,542 in 1820 to 30,490 in 1850 to 42,337 in 1890. (*Population U. S. Eleventh Census, 1890*, pt. 1, 35). According to the last census there were 123,063 inhabitants in the county. (*Population Fifteenth Census,* 1930, III, pt. 2, 484).

Ohio counties were laid out to fit the needs of an agricultural society of the nineteenth century. The last Ohio county was created in 1851 and there have been no changes in boundaries for over half a century. The counties now range in population from 10,000 to 1,200,000. Approximately 70 of Ohio's 88 counties may be considered rural. (R. E. Heiges, *The Office of Sheriff in the Rural Counties of Ohio*, Findlay, Ohio, 1933, 52). The average population is 30,000 but over half of the people live in eight large urban counties.

The county is a creation of the state for the execution of state policy and has such powers as the state confers on it. It has, however, had to provide an ever increasing number of local services similar to those rendered by municipalities and its legal status is therefore changing. The county eventually may become relatively less the agent of the state and tend to approximate the municipal corporation in the character of its activities and in its legal status. (Report of the Governor's Commission, *The Reorganization of County Government in Ohio*, 1934, 3, 28-29).

The board of county commissioners is the central feature of the structure of the county government. The functions of this board touch either directly or indirectly every other branch and department. The board is the agency in whose name actions for and against the county are brought. This board is empowered to determine certain policies for the conduct of county affairs such as adoption of the budget, establishment of services left optional by law, and the authorization of improvements. Thus in a limited sense it constitutes the legislative branch. The board also functions as the central administrative body although much of the administration, centered in other elective offices, is beyond its control. The county auditor was originally made secretary of the board and still functions as such in a majority of the counties. Later provisions of the law permitted the board to appoint its own clerk, thus removing this duty from the auditor. (*Ibid.,* 58-59).

There are three types of financial functions performed by county officers and employees: tax administration, handling of the fiscal affairs of the county, and the trusteeship of funds held for individuals in court procedures. The principal financial authorities are the board of commissioners, the auditor, and the treasurer. The commissioners levy taxes, appropriate funds, and authorize payments. The auditor's primary duties are the keeping of accounts, the issue of warrants, the valuation of real estate, and the preparation of the tax list. The treasurer collects taxes, receives and has custody of county moneys, and disburses upon warrant from the auditor. (*Ibid.,* 71).

There are three strictly clerical officers whose work consists mainly of the preparation and custody of records: recorder, clerk of courts, and the judge of the probate court. All three have some part in the recording of documents and instruments affecting the title of property and of other documents presented for record. The last two have as their principal duty the keeping of court records: the clerk of courts serving both as clerk of the court of appeals and the common pleas court, and the probate court looking after its own records. (*Ibid.,* 179).

It is the duty of the recorder to copy, index, and file documents authorized to be recorded in his office. These consist almost entirely of chattel mortgages and instruments affecting the title to real estate. (*Ibid.,* 180). The system of recording is prescribed by statute. With the exception of a few urban counties recording is done by typewriter with considerable use of printed forms. The photographic method of copying is now in use in Clark, Cuyahoga, Hamilton, Lucas, Montgomery, and Summit Counties.

The principal records of the clerk of courts are prescribed by statute. They include an appearance docket, an execution docket, a journal of the orders of the court, a complete record of case papers, a system of indexes, and the file of original papers. The clerk is responsible for a variety of non-judicial record work, of which the filing and indexing of automobile bills of sale is the major item. At present the clerk acts as the agent of the state for the sale of hunting and fishing licenses and also issues auctioneers' and ferry licenses.

The probate judge is by statute the clerk of his own court. The Constitution permits the combination of the probate and common pleas courts in counties of less than 60,000 population. In this case the judge of common pleas becomes *ex officio* the clerk of the probate division and two separate offices are retained for keeping records. Such mergers now exist in three counties: Adams, Henry, and Wyandot. (*Ibid.,* 182-183).

Listed below, with amendments, are some notable provisions adopted at the conventions of 1851 and 1912 which affected the organization of county government:

> "Laws may be passed to secure mechanics, artisans, laborers, sub-contractors and material men their just dues by direct lien upon the property, upon which they have bestowed labor or for which they have furnished material." (Art. III, sec. 33, 1851). "All nominations for elective, state, districts, county, and municipal offices shall be made at direct primary election or by petition as provided by law. . ." (Art. V, sec. 7,

1912). "The General Assembly shall provide by general law for the organization and government of counties, and may provide by general law alternative forms of county government. No alternative form shall become operative in any county until submitted to the electors thereof and approved by a majority of those voting. . . Municipalities and townships shall have authority with the consent of the county, to transfer to the county any of their powers or to revoke the transfer of any such power, under regulations provided by general law, but the rights of initiative and referendum shall be secured to every measure giving or withdrawing such consent." (Art. X, sec. 1, amendment adopted 1933). "Appointments and promotions in the civil service of the state, the several counties and cities, shall be made according to merit and fitness, to be ascertained, as far as practicable, by competitive examinations." (Art. XV, sec. 10. 1912). "Elections for state and county officers shall be held on the first Tuesday after the first Monday in November in the even numbered years." (Art. XVII, sec. 1, amendment adopted 1905).

The aim of the survey has been to make information available regarding the records which may have accumulated over a period of more than 130 years. Survey workers have not made a study of the functions of the county offices with a view toward recommending any reorganization of county government but in the report of the Governor's Commission (*op. cit.,* 186-187) recommendations were made bearing upon the records system as follows:

1.   County charters and optional forms of government should provide for a department of records and court service to take over the functions of the recorder and clerk of courts, the non-judicial record work of the probate court, and the functions of the sheriff as a court officer. (See also Heiges, *op. cit.,* 55-66).

2.   The issuance of licenses should be transferred from the clerk of courts to the department of finance.

3.   Wider use should be made of the photographic process of recording in larger counties.

4.   Legislation should be adopted permitting the destruction of chattel mortgages and automobile bills of sale after they have ceased to have effect.

5.   The requirements of the system of indexes of cases in the clerk's office should be eliminated from the code and only the index of pending suits and living judgments should be required.

6.   Provisions should be made in the rules of the common pleas court for service of process by mail and that method should be brought into general use. (See also Heiges, *op. cit.*, 60-61).

Following the report of the governor's commission, a new law (116 O. L. 132-133) was passed in 1933 permitting any county to adopt a charter or an alternative form of government, as provided in section 3 of Article X of the Constitution of Ohio, if it does not interfere with or restrict in any manner a charter which has been adopted by any municipal government. The electors may establish by charter provision a civil service commission or personnel department. In April 1935 (116 O. L. 134) the legislature also provided that the electors of any county may establish by charter provision a county department of health.

The legal development of the various county offices has been treated in a prefatory section preceding the inventory of the records of each office.

The records of Trumbull County are for the most part in good condition. Some, however, were damaged by the courthouse fire of 1895. Others were covered with a coating of dust and soot which had accumulated throughout the building. The offices, with a few exceptions are crowded, with no room for expansion, and the facilities for the use of the records are wholly inadequate at present.

At the outset, the research workers of the Historical Record Survey found the offices in a crowded condition; tons of unassembled records were piled haphazardly on the floor in the attic. The county commissioners realizing the condition that existed, appropriated $400 for the construction of shelving in the unfinished attic. The survey workers then dusted, shelved, and arranged many of the volumes.

However, the additional facilities proved inadequate, and at a regular meeting of the commissioners in May, 1936, a resolution was adopted to erect a modern fireproof building for the housing of the old records, to relieve the overcrowded conditions in the courthouse. The plans and specifications of the building for the archives were drawn, and a copy placed on file in the commissioner's office. (See floor plan of proposed building on page xxvi).

Most of the records of the county recorder are kept in two rooms on the second floor of the courthouse, and are with few exceptions in excellent condition. The bound volumes are kept on steel roller shelves and the unbound records in steel file boxes. Some of the outlawed chattel mortgages are stored in wooden and cardboard boxes in the attic, and a number of old volumes are in the state examiner's office on the fourth floor. Most of the latter have been transcribed and copies placed on file in the recorder's office. Those records in the attic are in poor condition. Accommodations for public use of the records are inadequate.

The county commissioners' office, situated on the north side of the courthouse, on the second floor, consists of three rooms including a waiting room. The rooms are well lighted and ventilated, and the accommodations and space are ample. Sixty percent of the records are found in the main business office and are in good condition. The bound volumes are kept on steel roller shelves and the unbound material in steel file cabinets. About 40 percent of the records of this office were brought out of the attic by survey workers and placed on steel roller shelves on the fourth floor. These older records are in poor condition.

The office of the clerk of courts is comprised of three rooms on the third floor, on the south side of the building. These rooms are well lighted and ventilated, but are crowded, with no additional space for expansion. The facilities for users of the records are inadequate. Two of the rooms contain approximately 70 percent of the records, which are in good condition. Most of the unbound records are located on the balcony in the main record room, while the bound records are kept on steel roller shelves below the balcony. Other records may be found in two rooms on the fourth floor over common pleas courtroom number one. In one of these rooms is stored a mass of records salvaged from the fire of 1895. These records are in very poor condition. Perhaps this office suffered a greater loss in the fire of 1895 than any other office.

The office of the probate court is located on the second floor and consists of three rooms on the northeast corner of the courthouse. The probate court also has the use of a room on the first floor. Seventy-five percent of the records of the probate court are housed in two rooms: the other records are located in the courtroom and in the attic. Except for dust, the records in these rooms are in good condition. The main filing room is well equipped with steel roller shelves and steel file boxes. Almost one-third of the space on the balcony is used for unbound records, the remainder for bound volumes. The office is crowded with no available space for expansion. Accommodations for users are inadequate.

The office of the prosecuting attorney and his assistant are located on the first floor, on the south side of the building, and consist of three rooms, including a waiting room. The latter houses practically all of the records. The rest of the records may be found in the prosecutor's office. The rooms are well ventilated, and there is ample space for expansion. The unbound material is kept in steel file cabinets, and all records are in good condition.

The office of the sheriff is located on the third floor adjoining common pleas court room number one, and consists of two well-lighted and well-ventilated rooms. About 80 percent of the records are stored in these rooms in steel file boxes and on wooden shelves. The remainder of the records are stored on steel roller shelves in the hallway on the fourth floor. All records are in good condition. Accommodations for users are very limited.

The county auditor's office consists of three rooms adjoining the auditor's private office and a room on the first floor near the south entrance to the courthouse. Eighty percent of the records are stored in these rooms in steel file boxes, steel file cabinets, or on steel roller shelves. The remaining 20 percent are located in a room on the fourth floor. With the exception of dust and soot, the records are in good condition. The rooms are now crowded and there is no room for expansion. Accommodations for users of the records are limited.

The treasurer's office is located on the south side of the courthouse. The room has adequate lighting and ventilation, but it is crowded and there is no room for expansion. Approximately 50 percent of the treasurer's records are kept in steel file boxes and on steel shelves; the remainder are stored in the engineer's drafting room on the fourth floor, or in the attic. These records in the treasurer's office are in good condition, but those in the drafting room and attic are in poor condition. The accommodations for users of the records are inadequate.

The office of the county engineer is located on the first floor at the west end of the building, and includes three rooms. A room on the fourth floor is also used as a drafting room. Lighting and ventilation in the rooms on the first floor are good, but the rooms are now crowded, with no room for expansion, and only limited facilities for the users. Ninety-five percent of the records are in the main drafting room on the first floor. The bound volumes are on wooden shelves and the unbound records are in steel file cabinets. Five percent of the records are stored in a wooden box in the attic.

The county board of education office is located at 410-11 Union Savings and Trust building, and consists of two rooms. Records are kept in both rooms. All records are in good condition. The rooms are crowded and accommodations are very limited.

The county board of health office is located at 508 Union Savings and Trust building, and consists of two rooms. All of the records kept there are in good condition.

The county board of elections is on the first floor, on the north side of the courthouse. There are two overcrowded rooms, in which practically all of the records are kept. The unbound records are in steel file cabinets, while the bound volumes are in a wooden cupboard. A few of the older records are stored in the attic, and except for dust and soot, all records are in good condition.

The office of the farm extension service is in the courthouse on the first floor, southeast corner. It consists of two small, overcrowded rooms, in which the records are kept in steel file cabinets and cardboard boxes.

The office of the soldiers' relief commission is on the first floor, north side of the courthouse. The room is well lighted and well ventilated. The records are in good condition, and the accommodations for users are adequate.

Although a distinct improvement has been made in the courthouse by survey workers, and steps have been taken to properly care for the records, it is not enough. There are many unimportant records, as well as old and broken furniture, which should be destroyed. This would provide much needed space for filing more important records. To relieve the present overcrowded conditions of the courthouse, the construction of the proposed modern, fireproof building is necessary.

PLATE X

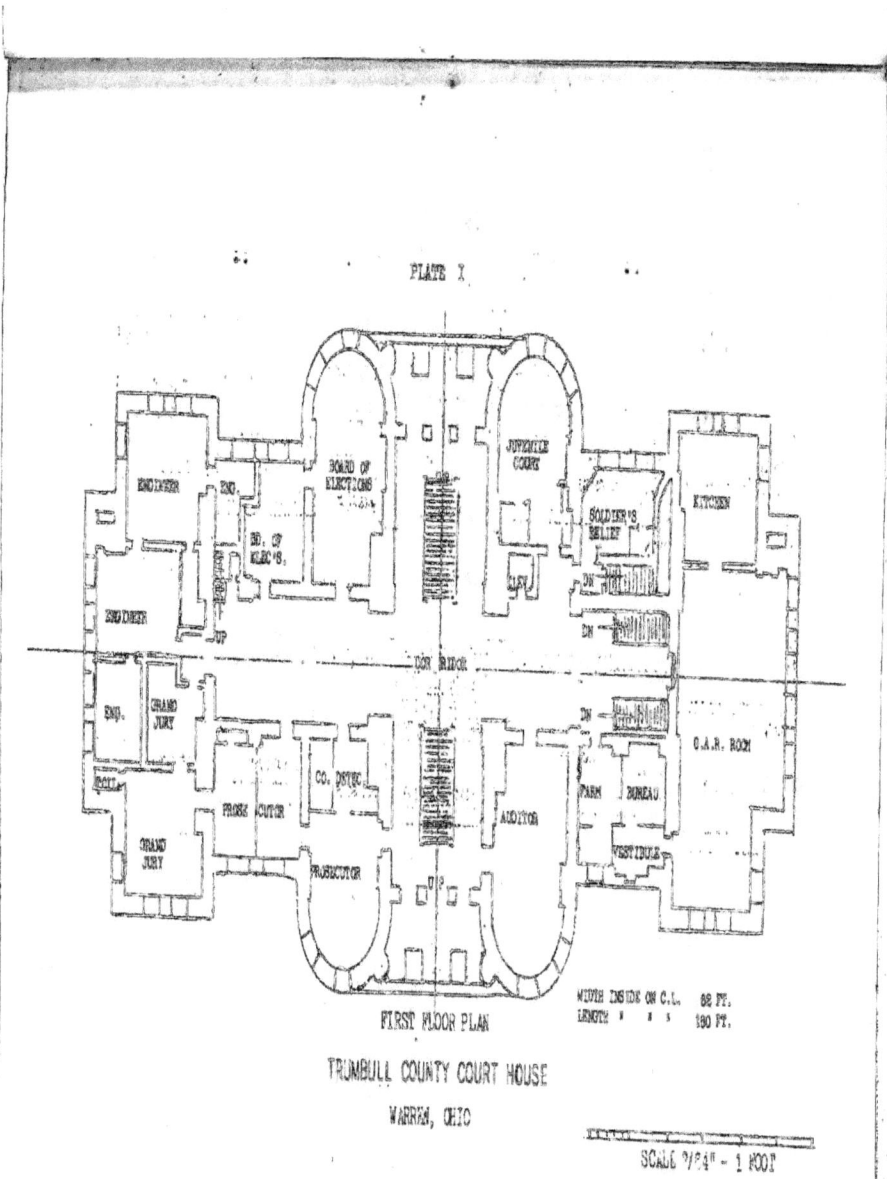

FIRST FLOOR PLAN

TRUMBULL COUNTY COURT HOUSE

WARREN, OHIO

SCALE 3/64" = 1 FOOT

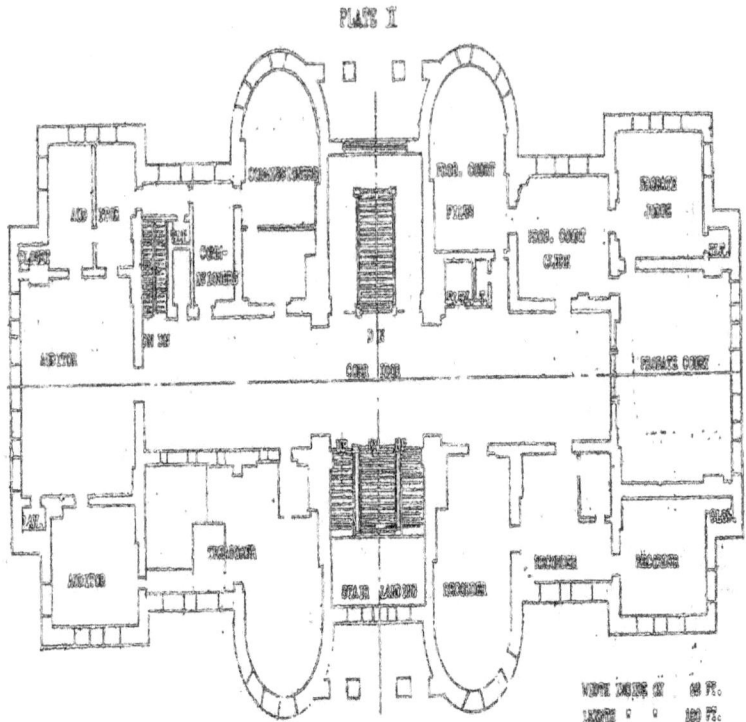

SECOND FLOOR PLAN
TRUMBULL COUNTY COURT HOUSE
WARREN, OHIO

PLATE II

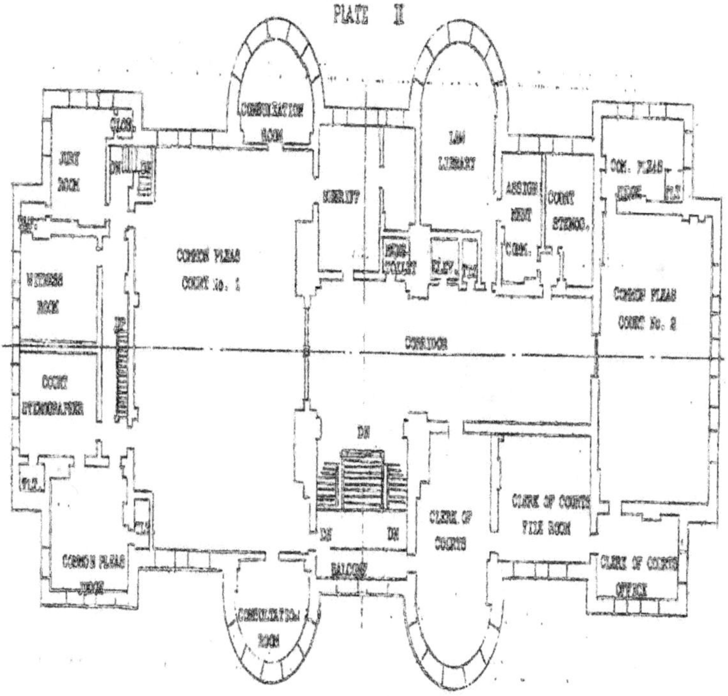

WIDTH INSIDE C.L. 62 FT.
LENGTH " " 180 FT.

THIRD FLOOR PLAN
TRUMBULL COUNTY COURT HOUSE
WARREN, OHIO

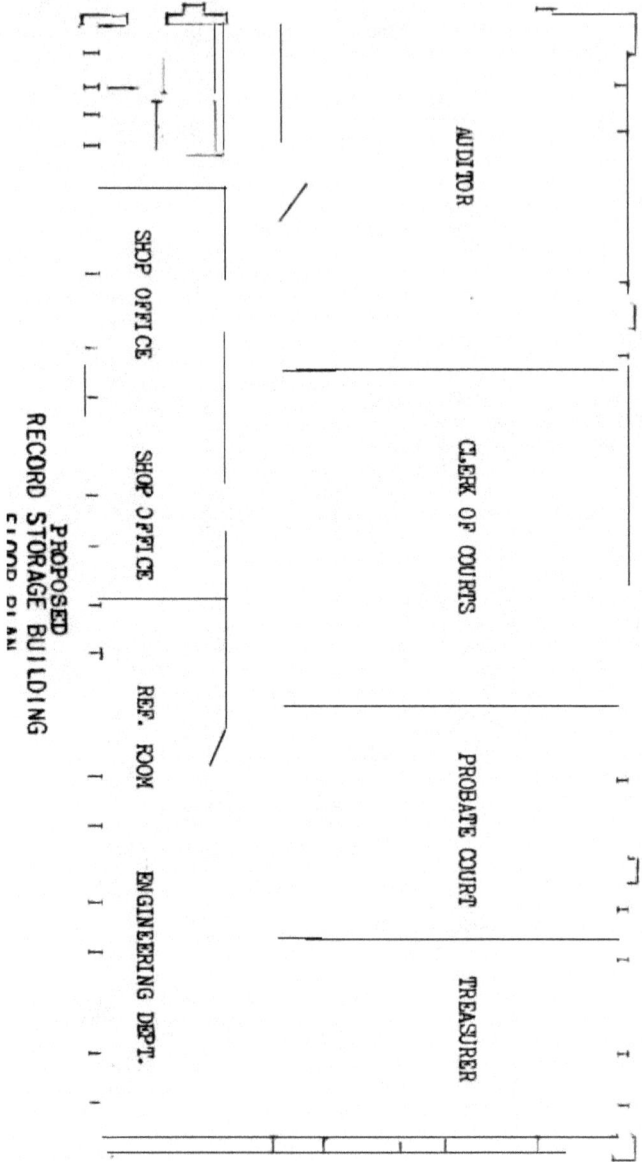

PROPOSED
RECORD STORAGE BUILDING
FLOOR PLAN

SHOP OFFICE

SHOP OFFICE

REF. ROOM

ENGINEERING DEPT.

AUDITOR

CLERK OF COURTS

PROBATE COURT

TREASURER

The office of county recorder, although not unknown as an early English institution for the registration of land titles, developed in colonial America where, due to the mobility of the restless pioneers, changes in land titles were frequent and some system was needed to protect purchasers against previous encumbrances. Public land registers, established in most of the colonies during the colonial period, were continued by the states following independence, and provided a model of land registration for the territory of which the present state of Ohio was then a part. Thus the office of county recorder was established by an act of the Northwest Territory passed on August 1, 1795. This act, adopted from the Pennsylvania code, provided for the appointment by the governor of a recorder in each county whose principal duty was the recording of deeds. (Theodore Calvin Pease, *Laws of the Northwest Territory 1788-1800.* Illinois State Bar Association Law Services, Springfield, 1925, 1, 197-199).

When Ohio entered the union in 1802 no constitutional provision was made for the continuation of the office, but the legislature during its first session passed an act providing for a recorder in each county to be appointed by the judges of the court of common pleas for a seven-year term. (1 O. L. 137). The recorder continued to be an appointive officer until 1829, when, by an act of the legislature, he became elective for a three-year term. (27 O. L. 65). The term remained at three years until the constitutional amendment of November 7, 1905, which provided for the election of all county offices in the even-numbered years. (*Ohio Const.* Art. XVIII, sec. 2). The term of office was fixed at two years, and so continued until the amendment of 1933, which extended the term of the incumbent until January 1937 at which time the recorder, elected at the regular election in November 1936, should serve a four-year term. (115 O. L. 191).

The first county recorder was directed by statute to record "all deeds, mortgages and conveyances of lands and tenements," lying within his county, and also all instruments and writings which were required by law to be recorded. (1 O. L. 137). In 1818 he was directed to record all plots and maps of newly laid out villages and divisions or subdivisions of towns and villages. In 1835 he was permitted, when authorized by the county commissioners, to transcribe from the records of other counties all deeds, mortgages, and other instruments of writing for the sale or conveyance of lands, tenements or hereditaments. (33 O. L. 8; 35 O. L. 10-11).

Since that time many new duties have been added besides those of recording land titles. The present practice of recording powers of attorney began in

1831. (29 O. L. 346). Successive acts in 1865, 1872, 1881, 1884, 1888, 1904, and 1923 added new duties in the recording of soldiers' discharges (62 O. L. 59), copies of certificates of compliance authorizing companies not incorporated under the laws of Ohio to transact business in the state, and certified copies of renewal as granted by such companies to their agents (69 O. L. 32), limited partnership agreements (78 O. L. 248), stallion keepers' liens (81 O. L. 179), partition fence records (97 O. L. 140), and federal tax liens. (110 O. L. 252). The recording of chattel mortgages and conditional sales, made compulsory in 1846, was made optional in 1878. (44 O. L. 61-62; 75 O. L. 519). Although the act of 1935 provided for the filing of chattel mortgages with the recorder exclusively, such filing was not made mandatory. (G. C. Sec. 8, 561).

In the latter part of the nineteenth century an important extension of the method of recording land titles was provided by an act of the general assembly. The "Torrens System," as provided by the act of 1896 (92 O. L. 220), was declared unconstitutional by the supreme court of Ohio as being repugnant to Sec. 16 of the bill of rights of the state constitution. (55 O. L. 575). The present act, passed in 1913 (amended in 1913 and 1915), provides for the examination of land titles by the recorder and the issuance, if the title proved to be held in fee simple, of a certificate of title by the courts. The official certificate becomes the title of ownership and is indefeasible. However, in the event an interest is found in the land, after the issuance of the certificate, a claim is allowed to the legal claimant from a fund created for that purpose at the time of registration. (G. C. sec. 8, 572-34 - 8,572-56; 106 O. L. 225; 115 O. L. 445-447). This system, although adopted by a few counties has proved unpopular because of the difficulty of replacing the traditional complicated system.

The recorder, like other county officials, has been required to keep record of the business of his office. Although records were prescribed in earlier years, it was not until the middle of the nineteenth century that the legislature enacted measures prescribing the form and contents of such records, looking forward to some uniformity in land registration. Since 1850 the recorder has been required to keep a record of deeds in which is recorded all deeds, powers of attorney, and other instruments of writing for the unconditional sale of land, tenements or hereditaments "shall or may be mortgaged" or otherwise conditionally sold; and a record of plats in which was to be recorded all plats and maps of town lots and of the subdivisions thereof, and of other divisions or surveyed lands, in like regular succession according to the priority of their presentation. (48 O. L. 64). Since 1851 the recorder has been required to keep a separate record of mortgages denominated as "Record of Deeds" and "Record of Mortgages." (49 O. L. 103). Ten years later saw the beginning of a separate record of leases in which the recorder was, and is, required to record all leases and powers of attorney for the execution of leases. (61 O. L. 55). The present practice of keeping a daily register of deeds and a daily register of mortgages had its beginning in 1896. In this record are recorded in alphabetical order the names of the grantors and all deeds and mortgages affecting real estate. (92 O. L. 268).

The present system of indexing, although indexes had been prepared in earlier years, had its beginning in 1851 and took practically its present form in 1896. (49 O. L. 103; 92 O. L. 268; 102 O. L. 277). At present the recorder, at the beginning of each day's business, is required to make and keep up a general alphabetical index, direct and reverse of all names of both parties of all instruments recorded by him. The indexes show the kind of instrument, the date, the range township and section, the survey number and the number of acres, or the lot and sublot numbers and the part thereof, of each tract or lot of land described in any such instrument of writing; the name of each grantor is entered in the direct index under the appropriate letter followed on the same line by the names of the grantee. The name of such grantee is entered in the reverse index under the appropriate letter followed on the same line by the name of the grantor. (G. C. sec. 2, 764).

Since 1859 the county commissioners have been authorized to provide sectional indexes to the records of all real estate in the county, beginning with some designated year and continuing through a period of years as maybe specified. (G. C. sec. 2, 766; 64 O. L. 256; 76 O. L. 49; 102 O. L. 277).

The present duties of the recorder do not differ, in the main, from those prescribed in the middle of the nineteenth century. His records, in large bulky volumes, are open to the inspection of the public, and are transferred to his successor.

Real Property Transfers

Deeds

1. DEED RECORDS
1795—. 399 volumes (26 volumes, A-Z; 373 volumes, 27-395)
Subtitled Quit-claim, Sheriff's Real Estate Devised by Will, Certificates of Transfer of Real Estate, and Corporation Deeds showing description of real estate, consideration (real and nominal), and mortgage deeds. The early volumes also contain lease, marriage, bond, mortgage, and survey records. A few of the early volumes have been transcribed. Chronologically arranged. For index see entry 2. 1795-1904, handwritten; 1905—, typed. Volumes average 600 pages. 20 x 14 x 3. County courthouse. Recorder's office, east and west walls.

2. INDEX TO DEED RECORDS
1795—. 60 volumes and duplicate set.
Alphabetical index of grantors and grantees showing date of filing, names of grantee and grantor, and volume and page reference to record; also description, lot number, name of township, tract, and range. Handwritten. Condition of 25 original volumes is poor. Volumes average 600 pages. 17 x 14 x 3. County courthouse,
    1795—, 60 volumes (transcribed), 35 volumes (originals), Recorder's office, east and south walls.
    25 volumes (originals), State Examiner's office, 4th floor.

3. DAILY REGISTER OF DEEDS AND MORTGAGES
1881—. 13 volumes.
Daily listing of all documents filed for recording giving date of receipt, document number, names of grantee and grantor, and type and kind of instrument. Numerically arranged by instrument numbers. Handwritten on printed forms. Condition poor. Volumes average 150 pages. 20 x 20 x 2. County courthouse.
    1881-1895, 8 volumes, State Examiner's office, 4th floor.
    1896—, 5 volumes, Recorder's office.

Leases

4. LEASES AND AGREEMENTS
1865-1935. 31 volumes (1-31).
Complete record of agreements regarding leases giving detailed description of property under consideration and amount involved. Some early leases are recorded in early deed records. 1865-1901, handwritten; 1902-1935, typed. Volumes average 640 pages. 20 x 14 x 4. County courthouse. Recorder's office, south wall.

5. INDEX TO LEASES AND AGREEMENTS
1865—. 5 volumes.
Alphabetical index of lessors and lessees listing date of filing and volume and page reference to record; also description, lot and sublot numbers, allotment, name of township, tract, and original lot. Handwritten on printed forms. Volumes average 200 pages.16 x 14 x 2.5. County courthouse. Recorder's office, west wall.

Mortgages

6. MORTGAGE RECORDS
1845—. 223 volumes.
Mortgage records including Home Owner's Loan Corporation mortgages giving description of real estate secured by mortgage. See entry 1for early mortgage record. For index see entry 7. 1845 - 1919, handwritten: 1920—, typed. Volumes average 640 pages. 20 x 14 x 4. County courthouse. Recorder's office, east wall.

7. GENERAL INDEX TO MORTGAGES
1850—. 20 volumes and duplicates of 17 volumes.
Alphabetical index of mortgagors or mortgagees showing date of filing, names of mortgagor and mortgagees, filing numbers, volume and page reference to mortgage record, name of township, and range and lot numbers. Handwritten on printed forms. Condition poor. Volumes average 600 pages. 17 x 15 x 3. County courthouse
    1850-1932, 17 volumes (originals). State Examiner's office, 4th floor.
    1850-1932, 17 volumes (duplicates). Recorder's office.
    1933—, 3 volumes, Recorder's office, west wall.

8. INDEX TO MORTGAGEES
1875—. 16 volumes.

Alphabetical index of mortgagees giving amount of mortgage, name of mortgagor, date of instrument, date of filing, instrument number, remarks, and date of cancellation. Handwritten on printed forms. Volumes average 250 pages. 17 x 15 x 2. County courthouse.

1874-1928, 12 volumes, State Examiner's office, 4th floor.

1929—, 4 volumes, Recorder's office, east wall.

9. RECORD OF DISCHARGE OF MORTGAGES
1891—. 10 volumes. (1-10).

Copies of Deeds of trust to satisfy mortgages. Alphabetical index in front of each volume. 1891-902, handwritten; 1903—, typed. Volumes average 450 pages. 20 x 14 x 3. County courthouse. Recorder's office, east wall.

Liens

10. LIEN RECORD
1869—. 11 volumes.

Records of mechanics' liens charged against property for labor and materials which have been furnished giving names of creditor and debtor, amount of claim, and filing date. Alphabetical index in front of each volume; also indexed by entry 11. 1869-1904, handwritten; 1905—, typed. Volumes average 480 pages. 18.5 x 12 x 3.5. County courthouse.

1869-1900, 5 volumes, State Examiner's office, 4th floor.

1900—, 6 volumes, Recorder's office, west wall.

11. INDEX TO LIEN RECORDS
1919—. 2 volumes (A-Z, A-Z)

Alphabetical index to property owners listing name of person holding lien, volume and page reference to record, date of entry, name of person lien is drawn against, filing number, description, lot and sublot number, name of township and tract. Handwritten on printed forms. Volumes average 200 pages. 17 x 15 x 3. County courthouse. Recorder's office, west wall.

12. RECORD OF RELEASE OF LIENS OF PARTIAL DISCHARGE OF REAL PROPERTY

1933——. 1 volume.

County treasurer's certificates of release listing name of person against whom lien was placed, date of filing, volume and page reference to personal tax lien record, and amount of lien. Alphabetically arranged. Typed on printed forms. 400 pages. 20 x 12 x 2. County courthouse. Recorder's office, east wall.

13. INDEX TO NOTICES OF LIENS AND DISCHARGES - SURETY TO RECOGNIZANCE

1929——. 1 volume.

Alphabetical index listing name of surety, name of defendant, amount of recognizance, instrument number and date of filing. Handwritten on printed forms. 252 pages. 20 x 15 x 4. County courthouse. Recorder's office, east wall.

14. FEDERAL TAX LIEN INDEX

1924——. 1 volume.

Alphabetical index by names of firms and corporations giving address, dates of filing and discharge, amount of tax, and penalties. Handwritten on printed forms. 100 pages. 17 x 15 x 1. County courthouse. Recorder's office, west wall.

15. INDEX TO PERSONAL LIEN RECORD

1932-1935. 1 volume.

Alphabetical index to personal tax liens amounted to $100 or more giving name and address of each taxpayer, date of entry, volume number and page reference of personal property tax duplicate, number of classification, amount of delinquent tax, penalty, and total amount due. Typed on printed forms. 250 pages. 14 x 10 x 2. County courthouse. Recorder's office, west wall.

Records of Registered Lands

16. REGISTERED LANDS, RECEPTION BOOK

1914——. 1 volume.

Daily receipt record of documents affecting registered lands. Numerically arranged. Handwritten on printed forms. Condition fair. 250 pages. 24 x 24 x 2. County courthouse. Recorder's office, north wall.

17. REGISTERED LANDS, RECORD OF LIENS, LEASES, TRUSTS, AND EXCEPTIONAL ESTATES
1917—. 1 volume.

Record giving description of real estate covered by leases, mortgages, mortgage assignments; and satisfaction of mortgages and mortgage deeds. Alphabetically arranged. Typed. Condition fair. 350 pages. 20 x 16 x 4. County courthouse. Recorder's office, north wall.

18. REGISTERED LANDS, REGISTER OF TITLES
1913—. 2 volumes.

Original certificates of titles to registered lands and transfer certificates of titles. Numerically arranged. Typed on printed forms. Volumes average 450 pages. 20 x 18 x 4. County courthouse. Recorder's office, north wall.

19. REGISTERED LANDS SURVEY
1839-1928. 2 volumes. (1844-1919, missing).

Plats and descriptions of surveyed registered lands. Alphabetically arranged. Typed and hand drawn. Volumes average 590 pages. 24 x 20 x 3. County courthouse. Recorder's office, north wall.

Maps, Plat Books, and Surveys

20. ATLAS OF TRUMBULL COUNTY
1874-1899. 2 volumes

Historical atlas showing maps, plats, historical data of Trumbull County, and individual sketches of its leading citizens. Alphabetically arranged. Condition poor. Volumes average 122 pages. 24 x 20 x 1. County courthouse. Recorder's office, north wall.

21. MAPS AND PLATS
1815—. 14 volumes.

Maps and plats of lots, allotments, and subdivisions of Trumbull County showing exact location and acreage. Prepared by various engineers. Marked by townships. Various scales. Sizes vary from 15 x 10 x .5 to 4 x 3 x 2. County courthouse. Recorder's office, west wall and in center file.

22. SURVEY RECORD
1798. 1 volume.

Record of survey of Johnston and Canfield townships (Canfield was formerly in Trumbull County). No index. Handwritten. 210 pages. 14 x 8 x 2. County courthouse. Recorder's office, south wall.

23. WESTERN RESERVE DRAFT BOOK
1795. 1 volume.

Resolutions and drafts of general assembly of state of Connecticut pertaining to Western Reserve; also record of original landowners, officers of Connecticut Land Company, and method of drawing or distributing lands in Western Reserve. This is a photostatic copy of the original which has been stored because of its condition. No index. 413 pages. 20 x 14 x 3. County courthouse. Recorder's main filing room, east wall.

24. DRAFT DECEMBER, 1802, REPORT OF COMMITTEE FOR CLAPING [SIC] PROPRIETOR OF CONNECTICUT LAND COMPANY
1802-1807. 2 volumes.

Information regarding surveys and reports of committee appointed by Connecticut Land Company which recommended that proprietor hold an interest of $13,333.33 1/3 of purchase price of this state. No index. Handwritten. Volumes average 20 pages. 16 x 8 x .5. County courthouse. Recorder's office, south wall.

25. PARTITION FENCE RECORD
1904-1934. 1 volume.

Record of line fences established showing exact location and agreements for upkeep between one or more owners. Alphabetically arranged. 1904-1920, handwritten; 1921-1934, typed. 640 pages. 18.5 x 12 x 3.5. County courthouse. Recorder's office, west wall.

Personal Property Transfers

26. CHATTEL MORTGAGES
1928—. 206 file boxes. (109858-228263).

Originals or duplicates of mortgages on chattel goods, conditioned bills of sale, bills of sale, wage assignments, and cancellation orders. There are 118,605 duplicates contained in file boxes. Approximately 115,000 duplicates contained in bundles and boxes dated prior to 1928 located in courthouse attic. Numerically arranged. For index see entry 28. 3.25 x 8.5 x 12. County courthouse. Recorder's office, north wall.

27. CHATTEL MORTGAGE RECORD
1877-1934. 2 volumes.
Record of special chattel mortgages recorded showing names of mortgager and mortgagee, amount of mortgage, instrument number, name of agent, date of recording, and description of property or goods. Alphabetically arranged. For index see entry 28. 1877-1921, handwritten; 1922-1934, typed.465 pages. 14 x 20 x 3. County courthouse. Recorder's office, west wall.

28. INDEX TO CHATTEL MORTGAGORS
1875—. 16 volumes.
Alphabetical index of mortgagers giving name of mortgagee, date of instrument, date of filing, amount secured, instrument number, remarks, and cancellations. Handwritten on printed forms. Volumes average 250 pages. 17 x 15 x 2. County courthouse.
1875-1928, 12 volumes. State Examiner's office, 4th floor.
1929—, 4 volumes. Recorder's office, west wall.

29. NOTICE OF INTENTION TO SELL AND TRANSFER STOCK OF GOODS
1909-1919. 1 volume.
Notices of intention to transfer stock of goods listing names, dates, and kind of goods. Alphabetically arranged. 1909-1910, handwritten; 1910-1919, typed. 300 pages. 20 x 14 x 1. County courthouse. State Examiner's office, 4th floor, east wall.

Corporations

30. CORPORATION RECORDS
1845-1934. 2 volumes.
Record of incorporation of townships, firms, and limits. Alphabetically arranged. Handwritten. Condition poor. Volumes average 450 pages. 16 x 10.5 x 2.5. County courthouse. Recorder's office, west wall.

31. PARTNERSHIP AND TRADERS' RECORDS
1884-1886. 1 volume. (Discontinued).
Record of individuals and partners engaging in business listing names, kind and place of business, and amount of capital invested by each. Alphabetically arranged. Handwritten. 425 pages. 20 x 20 x 2. County courthouse. State Examiner's office, 4th floor.

32. RELIGIOUS SOCIETIES
1845-1856. 1 volume.
Record of minutes and certificates of religious groups and societies applying for or receiving incorporation showing date of each application, name of organization, and location. No index. Handwritten. Condition poor. 140 pages. 16 x 10 x 1. County courthouse. State Examiner's office, 4th floor.

Business and Administration of Office

Fee Books

33. RECORD OF FEES
1907—. 37 volumes (1-37).
Daily record of all fees received showing date of filing or recording and amount of each fee collected. They are classified under chattels and other documents. Numerically arranged. Handwritten on printed forms. Volumes average 300 pages. 20 x 15. 2.5. County courthouse.

1907-1935, 34 volumes. State Examiner's office, 4th floor.

1936—, 3 volumes, Recorder's office.

34. STATEMENT RECORD
1893—. 6 volumes (1-6).
Annual statement of all fees collected and disbursed in recorder's office showing from what source and total amounts. No index. Handwritten on printed forms. Volumes average 110 pages. 16 x 16 x .5. County courthouse.

1893-1936, 5 volumes. State Examiner's office, 4th floor.

1936—, 1 volume, Recorder's office.

Grants of Authority

35. INDEX AND RECORD OF CERTIFICATES OF TAXES
1896-1933. 2 volumes. (1897-1931, missing).
Certificates of authority to an agent or agents to pay taxes on real estate. Alphabetically arranged. Typed. Volumes average 290 pages. 14 x 12 x 1. County courthouse. Recorder's office, west wall.

36. POWER OF ATTORNEY
1893—. 3 volumes.
Regulation forms listing names, addresses, and dates. Alphabetical index in front of each volume. 1893-1904, handwritten; 1905—, typed. Volumes average 525 pages. 18.5 x 12 x 3. County courthouse. Recorder's office, west wall.

Miscellaneous

37. MISCELLANEOUS RECORDS
1919—. 3 volumes (1-3).
Copies of probate and common pleas court orders, affidavits, amendments, bankruptcy proceedings, bills of sale, and other records not classified by law. Alphabetical index in front of each volume. Typed. Volumes average 575 pages. 20 x 14 x 3. County courthouse. Recorder's office, west wall.

SOLDIERS' AND SAILORS' DISCHARGE RECORD
1865—. 6 volumes (1-6).
Record of honorable discharges from the United States army and navy giving date, name, and length of service. Alphabetically arranged. 1865-1919, handwritten; 1919—, typed. Condition fair. Volume average 710 pages. 20 x 14 x 4. County courthouse. Recorder's office, south wall.

The local governmental system for the Northwest Territory comprising the present state of Ohio, established the office of county commissioners. This office, created by the territorial act of 1792, consisted of two appointed commissioners who were directed to compile a tax list, levy taxes for the county, and to draft plans for, and supervise the construction of a "court-house, pillory whipping-post, and several stocks." (Pease, *op. cit.,* 78.)

The governmental system established in 1803, under the first constitution of Ohio, made no provision for the office and its existence is due entirely to statutory enactment. By an act of the legislature passed in 1804, the territorial office was recreated and was to be composed of three members elected for a three-year term. (2 O. L. 150). Seven years later the commissioners were made a corporate body invested with the power to sue and be sued. They were required to keep a record of their proceedings; to assess taxes for the support of the county; appoint a county treasurer; and to supervise the construction of bridges. (8 O. L. 358). They were paid at a per diem rate. Moreover, during the same period they were given the task of constructing courthouses, jails, and offices for the clerk of courts, court of common pleas, the sheriff, the auditor, and the treasurer. (2 O. L. 156-157; 29 O. L. 315). Of these earlier duties the commissioners retain all but one: that of appointing a county treasurer. However, since 1831 they have been authorized to examine and compare the accounts of the county treasurer and county auditor and to examine the condition of county finances.

Besides the duties regarding construction and finance, the commissioners were given the task of constructing local highways when so authorized by the legislature. During the first thirty years of Ohio history the duties of the commissioners in this respect were local in nature. But as the system of road construction expanded they were given the additional duty of converting free turnpikes into state roads. (44 O. L. 74). During the forties and fifties private companies were authorized by the legislature to construct plank roads. (44 O. L. 126-127). When, in 1857, these companies were caught in the stringency of a financial depression, the county commissioners were authorized to purchase their holdings. If such a transaction was made, the transfer signed by the president of the company was to be deposited with the county auditor. (54 O. L. 198). In the seventies the commissioners, although earlier subjected to regulatory measures by the legislature, were prohibited from levying taxes for roads to exceed three mills on the dollar on the taxable property in the county. (69 O. L. 111). Later, in 1887, they were authorized to levy taxes not to exceed five mills on the dollar on all taxable property in the county for the maintenance and upkeep of roads which had been damaged by excessive wear or were damaged from other causes. (G. C. sec. 7, 419).

With the development of modern means of transportation, scientific principles were applied to road construction and maintenance. Although the county surveyor, now the county engineer, had in earlier years furnished the commissioners with statements for bridge construction, it was not until the latter part of the nineteenth century that they were authorized to utilize his scientific knowledge in road construction. (78 O. L. 285; 98 O. L. 245-247). At the opening of the present century the surveyor was directed to appoint a maintenance engineer, with the consent of the commissioners, to supervise the repairing of improved roads in the county. (108 O. L. pt. 1, 497).

Although the county commissioners have never been closely associated with the administration of criminal justice, their earlier duties regarding the construction of county jails qualified them, in the earlier period, for additional duties in this respect. During the middle of the nineteenth century the commissioners of Cuyahoga and Hamilton Counties were authorized to employ persons confined in the county jails on construction work. (37 O. L. 54). While this provision was repealed by the criminal code, adopted in 1853, other earlier functions applicable to all counties were continued. Since 1843 the commissioners have provided equipment and fixtures for places of incarceration, food, and clothing for prisoners; and appointed a jail physician. (41 O. L. 74; 87 O. L. 186). Since 1869 they have been authorized to offer a reward for the detection or apprehension of any person charged with a felony in the county. Moreover, since 1929, the commissioners, in any county where there is no workhouse, may, under certain conditions, release or parole an indigent person confined in jail. (66 O. L. 287; 113 O. L. 133). With the extension of modern crime into the rural areas, in the form of small-town bank robbing, the commissioners were given the duty of furnishing motorcycles to the sheriff and his deputies in an attempt to compete with the high-powered equipment is used by modern gangs. One of the latest functions, in this respect, is the contracting with radio stations for the broadcasting of descriptions of fleeing criminals. (G. C. sec. 13431-1).

Besides providing for those who have violated the laws of the county, the commissioners were given the duty of caring for persons, who, because of poverty, physical or mental defects, became a public charge. Since 1814 they have established and maintained "poor houses." (12 O. L. 298). Since 1913 they have been authorized, in any county containing a city which has an infirmary, to contract with the director of public safety for the care of the county's indigent. (G. C. sec. 2, 419-1). In 1933 the commissioners were designated as a board to administer the state law providing aid for the aged (115 O. L. pt. 2, 431-439). Two years later, in 1935, the commissioners were authorized to provide non-institutional support, care, assistance, or relief for the county's indigent and were authorized to establish a suitable agency or office for such purposes. (116 O. L. 134). Since 1908 the commissioners have been authorized to issue warrants for the relief of the blind in the sum of $400 per year. (G. C. sec. 2, 969).

In addition to furnishing financial aid to the civilian population the commissioners were authorized (1886) to levy a tax for the relief of indigent soldiers, sailors, or marines of the Civil War, or if such veterans were deceased, for their dependents. (83 O. L. 232). In 1919 the provisions of the original act were amended to include all veterans. (108 O. L. pt. 1, 633). The commissioners were authorized also, in 1884, to defray the funeral expenses of any honorably discharged soldier, sailor, or marine who died indigent. Ten years later the provisions of the act were extended to include the mother, wife or widow, of any soldier, sailor or marine, or any war nurse. (90 O. L. 177).

The humanitarian duty of caring for the county's children was delegated to the county commissioners. Since 1824 they have been authorized to establish and maintain children's homes. At the beginning of the present century, when the treatment of children was undergoing a remarkable change, they were authorized to place dependent and neglected children in private homes or institutions where they would receive food, clothing, medical and dental treatment. (109 O. L. 533). The development of a juvenile court system added new responsibilities. In order to completely segregate juvenile offenders from the regular criminal courts, the commissioners were authorized to provide a separate building to be known as the "juvenile court."

The commissioners, by the authority conferred upon them to construct public buildings, we're giving duties regarding educational advancement. Since 1871 they have been authorized to accept bequests for the construction of county libraries, and since 1913 to issue bonds, after submitting such questions to the voters, for the construction of libraries, or to contract with existing libraries for the use of people in the county. (G. C. sec. 2, 454; 2, 434-1; 110 O. L. 242). Moreover, during the same period they were authorized to provide and maintain civic centers in the county and to employ an expert director to supervise and administer them. (G. C. sec. 2, 457-4).

Other duties not closely related to the original duties of the Commissioners have been added from decade to decade. For example, in 1850 they were authorized to subscribe for one leading newspaper of each political party in the county and cause them to be bound and deposited with the county auditor as public archives. (48 O. L. 65). An amendment to the original act, passed in 1923, provided for the preservation of such newspapers for a period of ten years, after which they may be removed to the Ohio State Archaeological and Historical Society. (101 O. L. 4). Besides this, they have been authorized to promote historical research by appropriating annually assume not to exceed $100 to defray the expenses of compiling and publishing historical data for historical society's not incorporated for profit. (G. C. sec. 2, 457-1).

During the early years of the twentieth century the commissioners were given the duty of providing facilities for county sanitation, which, in previous years had been sadly neglected. In 1917 they were authorized to lay out, establish, and maintain one or more sewer districts within the county, and to employ a sanitary engineer to aid them in the performance of their duties. In counties having a population exceeding 100,000 the commissioners were authorized to create and maintain a sanitary engineering department. Since 1917 no sewer or sewerage treatment works may be constructed outside of any incorporated municipality by any person, persons, firms or corporations until the plans have been approved by the commissioners. (G. C. sec. 102-1; 107 O. L. 440).

Then, too, during the same period the commissioners were authorized to provide facilities for the treatment of tuberculosis. In 1913 they were empowered to appoint one or more visiting nurses to visit homes or places wherein there was a case of tuberculosis, and since 1917 have been authorized to establish tuberculosis dispensaries and provide by tax levies the necessary funds for their establishment and maintenance. (G. C. sec. 3, 153; 3, 153-5). Meantime they were authorized to cooperate with the commissioners of other counties for the establishment of a district tubercular hospital. (100 O. L. 87). Ten years later the commissioners in any county having more than 50,000 population, with the consent of the state department of health, were authorized to provide the necessary funds for the purchase or lease of a site and the erection and equipment or the lease and equipment of the necessary buildings there on for the operation and maintenance of a county hospital for the treatment of persons suffering from tuberculosis. (108 O. L. pt 1, 253; 109 O. L. 212; G. C. sec. 3, 148-1). The management and control of such a hospital was vested in the commissioners.

Finally the county commissioners have acted in a supervisory capacity over other county officials. Since the middle of the nineteenth century they have been authorized to compare the annual reports and statements made to them by the prosecuting attorney, clerk of courts, sheriff, and treasurer; take measures to rectify errors, correct discrepancies, and record in their journal the results of such examinations. (G. C. sec. 2, 504; R. S. 886; 48 O. L. 66). Such reports were filed with the county auditor who acts as secretary to the commissioners and has custody of their official acts and proceedings. Moreover, in the latter part of the same century the commissioners were given their present-day duty of visiting and reporting on the sanitary conditions and the treatment of inmates in hospitals, detention homes, private asylums or any other institution exercising a reformatory or correctional influence over individuals. These reports, filed with the county prosecutor, are open to the inspection and examination of the public. (G. C. sec. 2, 498; 92 O. L. 212).

The county commissioners offer a typical example of an office, which, designed primarily for an agricultural society, has expanded to meet the needs and requirements of modern society. At present the commissioners are elected for a four-year term. (108 O. L. pt. 2, 1300).

Journals and Reports

39. [COMMISSIONERS'] JOURNAL
1819—. 34 volumes.
Records and minutes of county commissioners pertaining to various appropriations and bills payable giving dates and amounts. 1818-1883, no index; 1883—, for index see entry 40. Handwritten. Condition fair. Volumes average 170 pages. 10 x 8 x 1 and 600 pages 20 x 14 x 3. County courthouse.
1819-1909, 21 volumes. Commissioners' file, 4th floor.
1910—, 13 volumes. Commissioners' office.

40. INDEX TO COMMISSIONERS' JOURNAL
1883—. 8 volumes.
Alphabetical index showing for each entry the date, journal number, volume number and page reference. Handwritten. 5 volumes average 638 pages. 20 x 14 x 3; 3 volumes average 500 pages (loose-leaf) 20 x 14 x 5. County courthouse.

     1883-1910, 3 volumes. Commissioners' file, 4th floor.

     1911—, 5 volumes. Commissioners' office.

41. ANNUAL REPORTS
1903-1905. 2 volumes.
Annual statements of expenditures made by County Commissioners showing amounts and purposes. Alphabetically arranged. Handwritten. Condition fair. Volumes average 100 pages. 20 x 18 x .75. County courthouse. Commissioners' file, 4th floor.

Bridge and Road Records

42. BRIDGE RECORD
18876-1892. 3 volumes.
Commissioners' record of accounts with various bridge companies for construction of bridges across streams in Trumbull County giving date, location, and cost. See entry 39 for bridge records after 1892. No index. Handwritten. Volumes average 629 pages. 20 x 14 x 3, County courthouse. Commissioners' file, 4th floor, storage.

43. ROADS LEADING OUTSIDE TRUMBULL COUNTY
1802-1862. 1 volume.
List of roads leading outside of Trumbull County showing where each road begins and ends. See entry 366 road records after 1862. Chronologically arranged. Handwritten. Condition poor. 360 pages. 14 x 8 x 1. County courthouse. Commissioners' file, 4th floor.

County Institutions and Relief

44. INFIRMARY RECORD
1913—. 3 volumes. (1-3).
Minutes and records of meetings of county commissioners pertaining to county infirmary. No index. Typed. Volumes average 250 pages. 18 x 12 x 1. County courthouse. Commissioners' office, northeast wall

45 DETENTION HOME
1931—. 1 volume.
Minutes and records of meetings of county commissioners pertaining to detention home. No index. Typed. 124 pages. 20 x 12 x 1. County courthouse. Commissioners' office, northeast wall.

46. TUBERCULOSIS RECORD
1928—. 1 volume.
Minutes and records of meetings a county commissioners pertaining to county tuberculosis hospital. No index. Typed. 217 pages. 20 x 12 x 3. County courthouse. Commissioners' office, northeast wall.

47. PAROLES
1924—. 1 volume.
Record of prisoners who have been paroled from county jail by county commissioners giving name of prisoner, date paroled, time served, and reason for parolling. No index. Handwritten on printed forms. 600 pages. 20 x 12 x 3. County courthouse. Commissioners' office, northeast wall.

48. BLIND RECORD
1908—. 3 volumes.
Minutes and records of meeting of county commissioners pertaining to blind relief giving name, date of application, and amount of relief granted. No index. 1908-1913, handwritten on printed forms; 1914—, typed on printed forms. Volumes average 238 pages. 20 x 12 x 2. County courthouse.
    1908-1913, 1 volume. Commissioners' file, 4th floor.
    1914—, 2 volumes. Commissioners' office, northeast wall.

49. BURIAL RECORD OF INDIGENT SOLDIERS
1885-1917. 2 volumes.

Record of indigent soldiers who served in Civil and Spanish-American wars and were buried in Trumbull County. Alphabetically arranged. Handwritten. Volumes average 350 pages. 16 x 10 x 1.5. County courthouse. Commissioners' file, 4th floor.

Miscellaneous

50. ANNUAL INVENTORY OF COUNTY PROPERTY
1935—. 2 volumes.

Record and description of all county-owned equipment listing identification mark, location, and valuation. No index. Typed on printed forms. Volumes average 100 pages. (loose-leaf). 16 x 14 x 1. County courthouse. Commissioners' office on counter.

51. SHEEP CLAIMS
1877-1917. 3 volumes.

Record of sheep killed by stray dogs and payment for same as authorized by county commissioners showing date, number of sheep killed, and amount of payment. See entry 39 for record of sheep claims after 1917. No index. Handwritten. Condition fair. Volumes average 300 pages. 20 x 12 x 1. County courthouse. Commissioners' file, 4th floor, storage.

52. SIDE PATH COMMISSION
1900-1901. 1 volume.

Minutes and records of the Side Path Commission regarding the construction and maintenance of bicycle paths in the county. The commission consisted of some of the county officials that other prominent citizens. No index. Handwritten. 290 pages. 16 x 8 x 1. County courthouse. Commissioners' file, 4th floor.

53. PROOF OF PUBLICATION
1916-1922. 1 volume. (Discontinued)

Record of notices published regarding special improvements which were to be made giving date, place of hearing, and location and kind of improvement. This is a scrapbook record made of newspaper clippings and advertisements. No index. 101 pages. 18 x 18 x 1. County courthouse. Commissioners' file, 4th floor, storage.

The office of clerk of courts, an ancient English institution originating before the time of Edward I (Sir Frederick Pollock and Frederic William Maitland, *The History of English Law Before the Time of Edward I,* 2 volumes, Cambridge, 1895, I, 184) was transplanted in America during the colonial period. The American Revolution made no radical change in the political heritage derived from England, and the office was continued by the states. The duties of the office were modified, however, due to a separation of administrative and judicial functions in the newer states, which under the English system had been combined.

The sections of the Ohio constitution of 1802, creating the judicial system for the state, provided for the appointment of a clerk of courts by the judges of the court of common pleas. He was to serve a seven-year term but was subject to removal by the appointing power for a breach of good behavior. (*Ohio Const., 1802,* Art. III, sec. 9). When, in 1851, a new constitution was adopted, the instrument made the office of clerk and elective one with a three-year term. (*Ohio Const., 1851* Art. IV, sec. 6). A constitutional amendment in 1905 provided that the terms of all elective offices should be for an even number of years, not exceeding for. In compliance with the amendment, the general assembly passed an act fixing the term of office of the court at two years. (98 O. L. 273). The term remained at two years until 1935 when it was extended to four years. (116 O. L. pt. 2, 1st sess. H. 603). The remuneration of the office was by fees until 1906 when the legislature prescribed a definite salary. (98 O. L. 98, 117).

The duties of the clerk of courts, like any other county officers, we're prescribed by Statute. The code of civil procedure, adopted in 1853, summarized the earlier duties and laid the basis for the present day duties of the clerk. The duties prescribed under this code were similar, in most respects, to those prescribed during the earlier years of the office. The clerk of courts was directed to issue all risks and orders for provisional remedies; endorse the date upon all papers filed in his office; keep the journal, record books, and papers appertaining to the court and record its proceedings. Although the clerk had kept records during the earlier period, he was directed to keep at least five books to be called the appearance docket, the trial docket and a printed duplicate of the trial docket, the journal, the record, and the execution docket. (511 O. L. 158-159; 78 O. L. 108; 78 O. L. 88; 86 O. L. 39; 86 O. L. 26). Eight years later, in 1871, the clerk was made official custodian of the law reports and books furnished by the state for the use of the court and bar, and was made liable for their destruction. (68 O. L. 109).

While the duties of the clerk is defined by the civil code of 1853 are still effective, other duties have been added by subsequent legislation. Thus for example, in 1858 the clerk was directed to receive notary commissions for record. (55 O. L, 13; 93 O. L. 406; 115 O. L. 117). He was required, also, to receive for record special police commissions (1867), trademarks (1883), partnership agreements (1894), index to judgments of the federal courts (1898), bills of sales of motor vehicles (1921), and certificates of judgments to operate as a lien (1935). (64 O. L. 60; 80 O. L. 195; 91 O. L. 357; 92 O. L. 25; 93 O. L. 285). On the other hand, many of the earlier duties of the clerk have been transferred to other departments of local government or have been abolished. The clerk issued marriage licenses, and ministers' licenses until 1851, after that date they were issued by the probate court. Moreover the clerk issued peddlers' licenses until the decade of the sixties, since that time they have been issued by the auditor. (58 O. L. 67). The practice of recording the names of black or mulatto persons in the office of the clerk to be used as certificates of freedom was, of course, discontinued following the War Between the States.

The clerk of courts was given other duties in addition to those of serving the court of common pleas and receiving documents for record. Since 1850 he has been required to report annually to the county commissioners of all fines assessed by the court in criminal cases, together with the names of the parties to each case, and the amount of money he has paid to the treasurer. (48 O. L. 66; 58 O. L. 69; 86 O. L. 239). Moreover, since 1867 he has been required to report annually to the secretary of state on the number of crimes committed in his county, the number of pending cases, together with the amount of fines collected. (64 O. L. 17). An act of 1927, amending the act of 1867, directed the clerk to report on any matters which the secretary of state might require, and to forward a duplicate copy of his report on crimein his county to the state board of clemency. The state board of clemency was abolished in 1931. (112 O. L. 203).

The county clerk of courts, like the county prosecutor, is one of the important persons in the judicial system. His importance and influence was not recognized until recent years.

District Courts (1851-1883)

Until 1851 the judicial power of the state of Ohio, in both matters of law and equity, was vested in the supreme court, court of common pleas, and justices' courts. The supreme court, during the first fifty years of Ohio history, served as a court of appeals, holding court in each county annually. When, in 1851, a new constitution was adopted, the judicial system was extended by the creation of district courts. These courts, composed of one supreme court justice and several common pleas judges in the district, were assigned original jurisdiction in the same matters as the supreme court, and such "appellate jurisdiction" as might be provided by law. (*Ohio Const., 1851* Art. IV, sec. 5-6). Thus by constitutional provision the courts were assigned original cognizance in *quo warranto, mandamus, habeas corpus,* and *procedendo.* (*Ibid.,* Art. IV, sec. 2). In addition to this, the legislature, in 1852, authorized the courts to issue writs of error, *certiorari, supersedeas, ne exeat,* and all other writs not specially provided by statute, whenever such writs were necessary for the exercise of its jurisdiction. The same act gave the courts appellate jurisdiction from the court of common pleas, in civil cases, in which the court of common pleas had original jurisdiction. (50 O. L. 69).

For the purposes of the district courts, the nine common pleas districts were apportioned into five judicial districts. At the sessions of the district courts, a judge of the supreme court was designated to preside; in case no judge of the supreme court was present, as was often the case, the judge of the court of common pleas in whose subdivision court was being held was directed to preside. (50 O. L. 69).

The district courts failed to function properly. Evidence seems to indicate that the ever-increasing number of cases coming before the supreme court made it difficult for the justices to attend the meetings of the district courts. Indeed, six years before the creation of the district courts, the supreme court dockets were overcrowded. In 1845 the legislature found it necessary to afford relief, temporarily, by prohibiting appeals from the courts of common pleas to the supreme court. (43 O. L. 80). A similar condition of overcrowding existed in the sixties. Thus, in 1865, the supreme court justices were relieved of the duty of attending the meetings of the district courts for that particular year. (62 O. L. 72). The judicial system had become slow and cumbersome. The courts declined rapidly after 1865 and were finally abolished in 1885. (82 O. L. 17-18).

Circuit Courts (1883-1913)

Following the complete collapse of the district courts and amendment to the constitution, adopted in 1883, made provision for circuit courts. "The circuit courts," stated the amendment, "shall be the successor of the district courts, and all cases, judgments, records and proceedings pending instead direct courts in several counties, shall be transferred to the circuit courts." (*Ohio Const*. Art. IV, sec 6). The courts were assigned the same "original jurisdiction with a supreme court, and such a pellet jurisdiction as maybe provided by law." Of the courts and the number of circuits was left to the direction of the legislature. Accordingly, in 1884, an act was passed dividing the state into seven circuits, and provision was made for the election of three judges in each circuit. (81 O. L. 170).

The circuit courts, in addition to the jurisdiction conferred upon them by Art. IV, sec. 6, of the constitution, were authorized by the legislature to issue writs of *supersedeas* in any case, and all other writs not specially provided for, nor prohibited by statute, when they were necessary for the exercise of jurisdiction. (81 O. L. 170). Moreover the courts were authorized to make and publish rules of procedure in their respective circuits, as they deemed expedient, not in conflict with the law or rules of the supreme court. (81 O. L. 170). On the other hand, the legislature directed that all cases taken to the circuit courts were to be entered on the docket in the order in which they were commenced, received or filed, and they shall, stated the law, "be taken up and disposed of in the same order." However, cases in which persons were seeking relief from imprisonment or persons who are convicted of a felony; cases involving the validity of any tax levy or assessment; cases involving the constitutionality of a statute; cases involving public right and proceedings in *quo warranto, mandamus, habeas corpus*, and *procedendo,* could be taken up in advance of their assignment or order on the docket. (81 O. L. 170).

Court of Appeals (1913—)

The judicial system of Ohio was again slightly changed in 1912. By an amendment to the constitution in that year the circuit courts were renamed court of appeals. "The courts of appeals," stated the amendment, "shall continue the work of the respective circuit courts and all pending cases and processes in the circuit courts shall proceed to judgment and be determined by the respective courts of appeals." (*Ohio Const*. Art. IV, sec 6). The judges of the several circuit courts were designated as the judges of the courts of appeals, and were directed to perform the duties thereof until the expiration of their terms of office. Vacancies, caused by the expiration of terms of office of the judges were to be filled by the electors of the respective appellate districts. The term of office was fixed at six years.

The jurisdiction of the court remained much the same as it had been in 1851. However, the court was assigned original cognizance in writs of prohibition (*Ohio Const.* Art. IV, sec. 6). And appellate jurisdiction in the trial of chancery cases. (*Ibid.,* Art. IV, sec. 6). However, certain restrictions were imposed upon the court. No judgment of a court of common pleas or superior court or other court of record should be reversed except by "the concurrence of all the judges of the court of appeals." (*Ibid.,* Art. IV, sec. 6).

At present the court consists of three judges in each of the nine districts into which the state is divided, each of whom shall have been admitted to practice as an attorney-at-law in the state for a period of six years immediately preceding his election, one of whom is chosen every two years, and holds office for six years beginning on the ninth day of February next after his election. The salary of the circuit court judge, fixed at $6,000 per year in 1913, was increased to $8,000 in 1920 and so continues. (103 O. L. 418; 108 O. L. pt. 2, 1301). The judges hold at least one session of court annually in each county in the district. (G. C. sec. 1, 514).

Court of Common Pleas

The court of common pleas, like many other county institutions, originated in England during the reign of Henry II. (Adams, *op. cit.,* 109, 134). Established in America during the colonial period, the office was continued by the states following the War of American Independence. The territorial act of 1788, establishing the American colonial policy in the Newer West in respect to the judiciary, contained sections authorizing the establishment of a common pleas court to be composed of not less than three nor more than five members. These members, appointed and commissioned by the territorial governor, were given jurisdiction in all civil matters. (Pease, *op. cit.,* 7).

When a constitution was drafted for Ohio, in 1802, preparatory to the state entering the union, provision was made for continuation of the territorial court. (*Ohio Const. 1802*, Art. III, sec. 1). The articles of the constitution, regarding the judiciary, provided for a court of common pleas to be composed of a president and associate judges. The members of the court, appointed by joint ballot of both houses of the general assembly, were to hold court in three judicial districts into which the state was to be divided by legislative action. (*Ohio Const. 1802* Art. III, sec. 3). The court was assigned common law and chancery jurisdiction in all cases as should be provided by law. (*Ibid*, Art. III, sec.3). To the court was assigned jurisdiction in probate and testamentary matters and in the appointment of guardians. Moreover, the court of common pleas and superior court were assigned original cognizance of criminal cases as might be provided by law. (*Ibid*, Art. III, sec. 4). Appeals might be made from the county commissioners, justices of the peace, and other inferior courts in civil cases to the court of common pleas. (*Ibid*, Art. III, sec. 3). Finally, the court was authorized to appoint a clerk. (*Ibid*, Art. III, sec. 6).

Since the provision of the constitution called for legislative action, an act was passed in 1803 interpreting the constitutional provisions. Under this act the court was given original jurisdiction in all cases in law and equity, when the matter in dispute exceeded the jurisdiction of the justices of the peace. The court was to take original cognizance of all probate, testamentary, and guardianship matters, and in all criminal matters exceeding the jurisdiction of the justices of the peace, except in cases where the punishment of the crime was capital. (1 O. L. 58). A year later the jurisdiction of the court of chancery was restricted to cases where the sum involved was less than $500. (2 O. L. 261). In 1807 this restriction was removed, and the court was given original jurisdiction in all cases cognizable by a court of chancery, subject to an appeal to the supreme court. (5 O. L. 117).

Meantime the court was assigned cognizance of criminal cases, wherein the punishment was capital, if the accused elected to be so tried. (4 O. L. 57). In 1810 the court was authorized to appoint a county prosecutor. (8 O. L. 165-167). The Chancery Act, adopted in 1824, conferred general chancery powers on the court. (22 O. L. 75).

Significant changes were made in the composition of the court and its jurisdiction during the middle of the nineteenth century. Under the constitution of 1851, the judges of the court of common pleas were made elective for a seven-year term. For the purpose of electing judges the state was divided into nine districts. The districts, of which Hamilton County constituted one, were to be composed of three or more counties. Each district, in turn, was to be subdivided into three parts, in each of which one common pleas judge was to be elected. Court was to be held in every district or county with such jurisdiction as should be fixed by law. (*Ohio Const. 1851*, Art. IV, secs. 3, 4). Provision was made for the removal of judges by a concurrent resolution of two-thirds of the members elected to each house. (*Ibid*, Art. IV, sec. 17).

The legislature, interpreting the constitutional provisions, made provisions for judicial districts, but left the jurisdiction of the court much the same as it had been in the earlier years of its existence. (50 O. L. 70). However, with the reestablishment of the probate court by constitutional provision, the court of common pleas was denied jurisdiction in cases of probate, testamentary, and guardianship matters. However the judgments and final decrees of the probate court could be reviewed by the court a common pleas on error. (51 O. L. 145). A year later, in 1852, the court of common pleas was given original jurisdiction of all crimes and offenses, except minor criminal cases, the exclusive jurisdiction of which was invested in the justices of the peace or other minor courts. (R. S. 13422-5; 51 O. L. 474; 52 O. L. 73).

During the same period the jurisdiction of the court, in certain counties, underwent a marked change. Thus in 1852, the criminal court of Hamilton County was reestablished and to it was transferred the criminal jurisdiction formerly exercised by the court of common pleas. The latter court was given original cognizance of civil matters. (50 O. L. 90). Shortly afterward the superior courts were reestablished in Cincinnati, and in Franklin and Montgomery Counties. (52 O. L. 34; 53 O. L. 38; 54 O. L. 37). Save in divorce, alimony, and bastardy cases, the courts had the same jurisdiction as the court of common pleas.

At the opening of the twentieth century sweeping changes were again made in the organization of the courts. By the constitutional amendment of 1913, the divisions and subdivisions as provided by the constitution of 1851 were abolished. Provision was made for the election of one or more common pleas judges in each county. (*Ohio Const.* Art. IV, sec. 3). Later provision was made for the selection of a chief justice of the court of common pleas. Under an act of March 13, 1923, in counties where there were two or more common pleas judges, they were authorized to designate one of their number as chief justice. The justice so designated by his colleagues was to serve in such a capacity until the expiration of his term, after which time the office of chief justice was to be an elective one. The elective section of the act was nullified by the supreme court on the grounds that the creation of a new elective official was unconstitutional. Accordingly, in 1927, and amendment was passed eliminating the elected feature of the act.

With the increased number of issues presented to the court of common pleas, the problem of judicial administration has become greater. This problem was solved in part by the creation of a chief justice of the court of common pleas who has been given the duties of superintending the business of the court, classifying it, and distributing it among the judges. Besides the duties enumerated the chief justice annually makes a report to the clerk of courts showing the work performed by the court and by each judge in the preceding calendar year. Moreover, he reports such other data as the chief justice of the supreme court may require. (G. C. sec. 1, 558).

Attempts have been made in recent years to improve the efficiency of the court by imposing stricter qualifications upon those who seek election to the bench. In 1917, an act was passed providing that a common pleas judge shall have been admitted to practice as an attorney and counselor-at-law for a period of six years preceding his election. (107 O. L. 164).

The court of common pleas has enjoyed a limited point of power. Until 1833, the court was authorized to appoint a clerk of courts. Since 1915, the court has appointed a jury commission (which see). Other appointments, authorized during the development of the office, are a court interpreter and a criminal bailiff. Since 1929, the court, in counties having a population in excess of 300,000 has been authorized to appoint one or more psychiatrists, psychologist, or other examiners or investigators who shall hold their offices at the will of the court, and received such compensation as the judge may determine, not exceeding the amount as may be appropriated by the county commissioners. (G. C. sec. 1, 541; 113 O. L. 467).

The records of the court of common pleas are deposited with the clerk of courts for safekeeping. He is made liable for the destruction of all law reports and books furnished by the state for use of the court and the bar. (68 O. L. 109).

Coroner

The office of coroner, next to the sheriff the oldest county office in America, had its inception in England during the latter part of the twelfth century. The coroner kept a record of the activities in the county, especially regarding criminal justice. At the end of the thirteenth century, it was his duty to make inquests whenever there was a sudden death in the shire, and the results were recorded in the coroner's rolls, and were presented to the justices when they made their eyre. (Sir Frederick Pollock and Frederic William Maitland, *The History of English Law Before the Time of Edward I.* 2 volumes, Cambridge, 1895, I, 519, 571; II, 588, 641).

This office, transplanted in America during the colonial period, was continued by the states following independence, and was adopted by the territory of which the state of Ohio was then a part. An ordinance of the Northwest Territory, published in 1788, authorized the governor to appoint a coroner in each county within the territory. This act, together with a supplementary act of 1795 adopted from the Massachusetts code, fixed the power and duties of the coroner. He was empowered to do any act which, by previous legislation had been delegated to the sheriff; he was given the ancient English duty of coroners in holding preliminary investigations over the bodies of all persons found within his county who were believed to have died by violence or casualty. (Theodore Calvin Pease, *The Laws of the Northwest Territory 1798-1800*. Illinois State Bar Association, Law Series, I, 24-25; 372-375).

The Ohio Constitution of 1802 continued the historic office, making it elective for a two-year term. (*Ohio Const., 1802*, Art. VI, sec. I). A statute of 1805 defined the duties and authority of a coroner which, in the main, were comparable to those prescribed in the territorial code. He was, however, denied the privilege of concurrent jurisdiction with the sheriff. (3 O. L. 156-191). The act further provided that the coroner should receive his remuneration from fees; that if the office of sheriff were to become vacant due to death, resignation or otherwise, the coroner was to execute temporarily the duties of the sheriff. (3 O. L. 158-161). The latter provision remained active until its abrogation in 1887. (84 O. L. 208-210).

The constitution of 1851 and the constitution amendments of 1912 left the duties of the coroner unchanged and not until recent years, when he became an aide in the scientific detection of criminals, have any laws been passed which materially affected his office. By the legislative act of 1921 in all counties having a population of 100,000 or more, only licensed physicians were eligible to the office and at the same time the coroner was made official custodian of the morgue. (109 O. L. 43-44). In 1927 an act was passed, apparently designed to attract more highly trained physicians, which set the salary of the coroner at $6,000 per year in all counties having a population of 400,000 or more inhabitants, and authorized him to appoint one stenographer, a secretary, and three assistant custodians of the morgue. (112 O. L. 204-205). Two years later the coroner was empowered to appoint apologist to serve as deputy coroner. The deputy was directed to make chemical tests and to conduct autopsies. (113 O. L. 497). In 1936 the tenure of office was extended from two to four years. (G. C. sec. 2, 823).

Jury Commission

Pursuant to an act of the general assembly April 23, 1894, the judges of the court of common pleas, in counties having a population of not less than 33,000 nor more than 50,000, were empowered to appoint four residents of the county to serve as a jury commission for a term of one year. They were to receive compensation of $3.00 per day. It was the duty of this commission to determine the qualifications and fitness of persons to be selected as jurors. (91 O. L. 176).

An amendment in 1913 provided for the appointment and designation of juror commissioners to act as assignment commissioners. (103 O. L. 513). The act as amended in 1915 provided that in every county a jury commission of two resident electors shall be appointed, neither of whom shall be an attorney at law, nor of the same political party.

The Jury Code which became effective August 2, 1931 was in large part based on the work of the jury commission in Cuyahoga County and provided for a permanent jury commission of the same number and qualifications as previously provided for, to hold office at the pleasure of the judges of the common pleas court, and to meet and select prospective jurors, both grand and petit, for the ensuing year from a list of electors provided by the board of elections. (114 O. L. 213).

The jury commission selects perspective jurors for civil and criminal cases as well as for the grand jury. It selects jurors for the probate court, juvenile court, other minor courts, and all cities and villages where there are no established municipal courts.

Supreme Court

54. SUPREME COURT JOURNAL
1808-1832. 1 volume.

Record of cases tried in supreme court when convening in Trumbull County showing names of plaintiff and defendant, date of hearing, names of attorneys appearing in case, disposition of case, and signatures of judges. No index. Handwritten. 268 pages. 16 x 10 x 2. County courthouse. Clerk's office, balcony, east wall.

55. SUPREME COURT RECORD
1837-1857. 2 volumes.
Record of cases tried in supreme court when convening in Trumbull County showing names of plaintiff and defendant, date of hearing, names of attorneys, and signature of clerk. No index. Handwritten. Volumes average 475 pages. 20 x 14 x 2. County courthouse. Clerk's office, balcony, east wall.

56. CRIMINAL JOURNAL
1885-1895. 1 volume.
Records and mandates of Supreme Court of Ohio when convening in Trumbull County showing names of plaintiff and defendant, date of hearing, and decision of court in case. Alphabetical index in back of volume. Handwritten. 600 pages. 20 x 14 x 3.5. County courthouse. Clerk's office, east wall.

District Court

57. DISTRICT COURT EXECUTION DOCKET
1849-1882. 1 volume.
Record of district court findings and mandates in chancery and civil cases. Alphabetically arranged. Handwritten. 540 pages. 15 x 12 x 2.5. County courthouse. Clerk's office, east wall.

58. DISTRICT COURT DOCKET
1878-1884. 1 volume.
List of causes for trial in district court showing names of plaintiff and defendant, names of attorneys, and disposition of case. Chronologically arranged. Handwritten on printed forms. 278 pages. 18 x 10 x 2. County courthouse. Clerk's room, 4th floor.

59. DISTRICT COURT RECORD
1853-1885. 3 volumes (1856-1879, missing).
Record of district court proceedings showing date, names of plaintiff and defendant, and name of judge. Missing volumes were destroyed in courthouse fire of 1895. No index. Handwritten. Volumes average 500 pages. 18 x 14 x 3. County courthouse. Clerk's office, east wall.

Circuit Court

60. CIRCUIT COURT APPEARANCE DOCKET
1882-1912. 2 volumes.
Record showing names of witnesses and attorneys; also costs and dates. Alphabetically arranged. Handwritten on printed forms. Condition fair. Volumes average 400 pages. 2 x 14 x 2. County courthouse. Clerk's office, east wall.

61. CIRCUIT COURT DOCKET
1885-1912. 2 volumes.
List of cases tried in circuit court and a record of the disposition of the cases. Chronologically arranged. Handwritten on printed forms. Condition fair. Volumes average 150 pages. 17 x 9 x 1. County courthouse. Clerk's room, 4th floor, north wall.

62. CIRCUIT COURT RECORD
1887-1912. 3 volumes. (2-4)
Records and petitions of circuit court showing names of plaintiff and defendant, date of filing, docket and page numbers, names of attorneys, signature of clerk, and sheriff's return. No index. 1887-1906, handwritten; 1907-1912, typed. Volume Savage 640 pages. 20 x 14 x 3. County courthouse. Clerk's office, balcony, east wall.

63. CIRCUIT COURT JOURNAL
1895-1912. 2 volumes
Records and proceedings of circuit court showing date of trial, names of plaintiff and defendant, supreme court mandates, and signature of clerk. Alphabetical index in front of each volume. 1895-1910, handwritten; 1911-1912, typed. Condition fair. Volumes average 585 pages. 20 x 14 x 3. County courthouse. Clerk's office, balcony, east wall.

64. CIRCUIT COURT, RESTORED RECORD
1903. 1 volume.
Due to the courthouse fire in 1895, certain papers and records were partially or totally destroyed and as the result in these cases the circuit court reviewed and caused them to be restored. This record shows the names of plaintiff and defendant,

date of hearing, name of attorney, and docket and page numbers. No index. Handwritten. 500 pages. 20 x 14 x 3.5. County courthouse. Clerk's office, balcony, east wall.

Court of Appeals

65. COURT OF APPEALS DOCKET
1913-1928. 2 volumes
Record of cases tried before the court of appeals getting names of parties and attorneys in the case, statement of proceedings, and common pleas journal and page numbers. Alphabetical index in front of each volume. Handwritten. Condition fair. Volumes average 100 pages. 18 x 12 x 2. County courthouse. Clerk's office.

66. COURT OF APPEALS APPEARANCE DOCKET
1913—. 2 volumes.
Appearance record of cases appealed from the lower courts giving case number, date, and names of plaintiff and defendant. Alphabetically arranged. Handwritten on printed forms. Volumes average 500 pages. 20 x 14 x 3.5. County courthouse, Clerk's office, east wall.

67. COURT OF APPEALS JOURNAL
1912—. 3 volumes.
Records and proceedings of the court of appeals showing date of hearing, names of plaintiff and defendant, and decision of the court. For index see entry 88. Typed. Volumes average 600 pages. 20 x 14 x 3.5. County courthouse. Clerk's office, east wall.

68. COURT OF APPEALS RECORDS
1920—. 37 file boxes.
Transcripts of docket and journal entries of court of appeals showing case, dockets, and page numbers of the record; also names of plaintiff, defendant, and attorney and date of filing. Many of the early records were destroyed in courthouse fire of 1895. Some of the salvaged records are stored in no particular order. Numerically arranged. For index the entry 88. File boxes, 8 x 4 x 12 and 12 x 10 x 20. County courthouse.

1920-1927, 4 file boxes. Clerk's room, 4th floor, e. wall.
1928—, 33 file boxes. Clerk's office, balcony, west wall.

Court of Common Pleas

Dockets and Clerk's Entries

69. COMMON PLEAS COURT (Bar List)
1841-1873. 8 volumes.
Record of causes for trial listing date of each assignment, kind of case, and names of plaintiff, defendant, and attorney. Chronologically arranged. Handwritten on printed forms. Condition fair. Volumes average 140 pages. 16 x 10 x 1. County courthouse. Clerk's room, 4th floor, north wall.

70. CRIMINAL DOCKET
1804—. 29 volumes
Clerk's calendar of criminal cases tried in common Police Court showing names of plaintiff, defendant, attorney, date, and case number. Alphabetical index in front of each volume. 1804-1923, handwritten; 1924—, typed on printed forms. Volumes average 50 pages. 6 x 6 x 1, and 600 pages 20 x 14 x 3.5. County courthouse.
1804-1869, 15 volumes. Clerk's room, 4th floor.
1870—, 14 volumes. Clerk's office, east wall.

71. LIEN DOCKET
1921-1929. 5 file boxes.
Transcripts from civil docket showing docket and page numbers, executions on transcripts, and sheriff's returns; also names of plaintiff, defendant, and attorneys. Numerically arranged. Handwritten on printed forms. 4 x 8 x 12. County courthouse. Clerk's office, balcony, west wall.

72. COMMON PLEAS ISSUE DOCKET
1808-1859. 16 volumes.
Record of cases tried in common Police Court showing date, names of plaintiff and defendant, kind of case, and disposition of case. Chronologically arranged. And written. Condition fair. Volumes average 225 pages. 17 x 9 x 1.5. County courthouse. Clerk's room, 4th floor.

Records of Trials

73. COMMON PLEAS COURT RECORDS
1806—. 886 file boxes and uncounted bundles.
Petitions giving case number, names of plaintiff and defendant, cost, record, docket and page numbers, summons, bearing date received and returned, and decision of court in each case. Besides the 886 file boxes there are a number of boxes (wood and cardboard), baskets, and other types of containers which it is impossible to count. There is no system of filing for early records. Later records are numerically arranged. For index entry 88. Handwritten and typed on printed forms. File boxes average 8 x 4 x 12 to 12 x 10 x 20. County courthouse.
   1805-1893, 140 file boxes. Clerk's room, 4th floor, south wall.
   1893-1928, 211 file boxes, uncounted bundles. Clerk's office, north wall.
   1928—, 535 file boxes. Clerk's office, northwest wall,

74. COMMON PLEAS JOURNAL
1808—. 103 volumes. (1-103).
Records and decisions of common pleas court cases showing date, names of plaintiff and defendant, name of attorney, and case number. Alphabetically arranged. 1808-1914, handwritten; 1915—, typed. Condition fair. Volumes average 550 pages. 20 x 14 x 3,5, County courthouse. Clerk's office, balcony, east wall.

75. COURT OF ASSOCIATE JUDGES
1808-1844. 1 volume.
Common pleas court records of proceedings, mostly records of licenses granted by associate judges to operate taverns, places of public entertainment, and mercantile establishments. No index. Handwritten. Condition poor. 200 pages. 12 x 6 x 1. County courthouse. Clerk's room, 4th floor, north wall.

76. COMMON PLEAS RECORD
1819—. 259 volumes. (7-13, 15-266) (1895 missing).
Record of proceedings of common pleas court showing the date pleas, names of plaintiff and defendant, docket and page numbers, and name of attorney. For index see entry 88. 1818-1909, handwritten; 1910— typed. Condition fair. Volumes average 550 pages. 20 x 14 x 3.5. County courthouse. Clerk's office, north and east walls.

77. CHANCERY RECORDS
1842-1852. 8 volumes. (5-12) (volumes 1-4 were destroyed in courthouse
    fire of 1895).

Records of proceedings of common pleas court (chancery sittings); also petitions
in court actions showing names of plaintiff and defendant, date of hearing, and
mandates from supreme court. No index. Handwritten. Volumes average 475 pages.
20 x 14 x 3. County courthouse. Clerk's office, balcony, east wall.

78. RESTORED RECORDS
1855-1866. 1 volume.

Copies of records which were partially destroyed in courthouse fire of 1895. Cases
were reviewed and settled in common pleas court. No index. Handwritten. 600
pages. 18 x 14 x 3.5. County courthouse. Clerk's office, east wall.

79. OLD CRIMINAL RECOGNIZANCES
1909-1931. 2 file boxes

Common pleas records and recognizances of accused. For index see entry 88.
Handwritten. 4 x 8 x 12. County courthouse. Clerk's office, west wall.

Clerk's General Records

Dockets and Clerk's Entries

80. APPEARANCE DOCKET
1804— 114 volumes.

Record of persons summoned to appear at court trials. Indexed by tabs by court
terms. Handwritten. Volumes average 400 pages. 18 x 13 x 2.75. County
courthouse,

    1804-1856, 35 volumes. Clerk's room, 4th floor.

    1857—, 79 volumes. Clerk's office.

81. COURT DOCKET
1891-1913. 68 volumes.

Record of causes for trial showing case number, names of plaintiff and defendant,
date, name of attorney, kind of action, and disposition of case. Chronologically

arranged. Handwritten on printed forms. Volumes average 79 pages. 18 x 9 x .75. County courthouse. Clerk's room, 4th floor, north wall.

82. CIVIL TRIAL DOCKET
1879. 1 volume.
Assignment of civil cases to be tried in court listing the names of plaintiff and defendant. No index. Handwritten on printed forms. 280 pages. 18 x 10 x 2. County courthouse. Clerk's room, 4th floor, north wall.

83. CRIMINAL TRIAL DOCKET
1874-1914. 12 volumes.
Assignment docket of criminal cases showing names of plaintiff and defendant, date, charge, name of attorney, and disposition of case. Indexed by tabs by court terms. Handwritten on printed forms. Condition fair. Volumes average 294 pages. 16 x 8 x 1. County courthouse. Clerk's room, 4th floor, north wall.

84. LIEN DOCKET
1856-1935. 10 volumes. (1-10).
Record of transcripts from justices of peace dockets and personal property judgments giving case number, date, names of plaintiff and defendant, and amount of judgment. Alphabetically arranged. Handwritten. Condition fair volumes average 600 pages. 16 x 12 x 2.5. County courthouse. Clerk's office, east wall.

85. JUDGEMENT LIEN DOCKET
1935—. 1 volume.
Certified list of judgments granted by court showing case number, names of plaintiff and defendant, and name of attorney appearing. Alphabetically arranged. Typed. 176 pages. 20 x 14 x 1. County courthouse. Clerk's office, east wall.

86. PRAECIPE BOOK
1834—. 14 volumes.
Record of orders issued by county clerk to the sheriff showing case number and date of issuance. No index. Handwritten on printed forms. Volumes average 396 pages. 14 x 10 x 2. County courthouse.
    1834-1885, 3 volumes, Clerk's room, 4th floor.
    1886—. 11 volumes. Clerk's office, east wall.

87. TRIAL DOCKETS
1808-1876. 11 volumes

Assignment record of cases to be tried in court listing the date, names of plaintiff and defendant, cause for trial, and disposition of case. Chronologically arranged. Handwritten on printed forms. Volumes average 320 pages. 18 x 10 x 2. Condition fair. County courthouse. Clerk's room, 4th floor, north wall.

88. GENERAL INDEX
1819—.13 volumes.

Alphabetical index to court records showing record book number, names of plaintiffs and defendants, and page and docket numbers. 1818-1925, handwritten; 1926—, handwritten and typed on printed forms. Volumes average 520 pages. 17.5 x 12 x 2.75. County courthouse. Clerk's office, east wall.

Records of Trial and Court Orders

89. CRIMINAL CASES (Recorded)
1914—. 58 file boxes.

Transcripts from the criminal docket showing the case, docket, and page numbers; also the names of plaintiff and defendant, date of trial, and amount of bond. Many of the early records were destroyed in courthouse fire of 1895 and many of the others have never been refiled in any particular order. Numerically arranged. Typed on printed forms. File boxes 8 x 4 x 12 and 12 x 10 x 20. County courthouse.

1931—, 17 file boxes Clerk's office, balcony, south wall.
01914-1930, 41 file boxes, Clerk's room, 4th floor, south wall.

90. INDEX TO PENDING SUITS AND LIVING JUDGEMENTS
1878—. 10 vols.

Alphabetical index listing names of persons, pending suits and case numbers, living judgments and case numbers, and living execution numbers. Handwritten on printed forms. Volumes average 644 pages. 20 x 14 x 2.5. County courthouse. Clerk's office, filing cabinet, east wall.

91. CASES TO BE RECORDED
1935—. 42 file boxes.

Court orders and records to be recorded showing case, docket, and page number;

also names of plaintiffs and defendants. Numerically arranged. Typed. 8 x 4 x 12. County courthouse. Clerk's office, west wall.

92. DEPOSITIONS DISPOSED OF CASES
1920-1928. 7 file boxes.
Depositions of witnesses taken in court cases. Numerically arranged. Handwritten. 4 cx 8 x 12. County courthouse. Clerk's office, west wall.

93. JURY BOOK
1887—. 4 volumes (1925-1928, missing).
List of jurors in court cases showing names of plaintiff and defendant, date and time jury was sworn in, court-term, jury's verdict, and date and time jury was discharged. No index. Handwritten on printed forms. Volumes average 498 pages. 14 x 8 x 1.75. County courthouse.
> 1887-1925, 3 volumes. Clerk's office, east wall.
> 1936—, 1 volume. Common pleas courtroom number 1.

94. JURY TIME BOOK
1856—. 5 volumes. (1918-1929, missing).
List of jurors surgeon showing their names, dates, and total number of days served. No index. Handwritten on printed forms. Condition poor. Volumes (1856-1886) Average 60 pages. 18 x 12 x 1; (1887—) 234 pages. 20 x 14 x 1. County courthouse.
> 1856-1917, 4 volumes, Clerk's room, 4th floor.
> 1930—, 1 volume, Clerk's office.

Corporations

95. PARTNERSHIP RECORD
1895—. 1 volume.
Register of persons forming business Partnerships giving names of persons and certificate numbers. Alphabetically arranged. Handwritten. Condition poor. 100 pages. 20 x 12 x 1. County courthouse. Clerk's office, east wall.

96. TRADE-MARK RECORD
1926-1934. 1 volume.

Record of persons or firms owning trademarks giving name of person or firm, date, and description of trademark. Alphabetically arranged. Handwritten on printed forms. 100 pages. 16 x 8 x .5. County courthouse. Clerk's office, east wall.

Elections

97. MAYOR'S CERTIFICATES OF ELECTION RECORD
1876-1902. 1 volume.

Certificates of mayor's elections. Alphabetical index. Handwritten. 456 pages. 19 x 8 x 23. County courthouse. Clerk's room, 4th floor, north wall.

Business and Administration of Office

Cash Books and Fee Books

98. REAL ESTATE LEVIES
1848—. 11 volumes. (1-11).

Real estate ordered sold by the court and amount of levees they're on showing date, location, and reason for selling. Alphabetically arranged. 1848-1923, handwritten; 1924—, typed. Condition fair. Volumes average 600 pages. 20 x 12 x 3.5. County courthouse. Clerk's office, east wall.

99. CASH BOOK
1855—. 35 volumes.

Record of all money received in court cases showing date, case number, title of case, from whom received, total amount, total deposited, and date deposited. No index. Handwritten on printed forms. Volumes average 260 pages. 18 x 16 x 2. County courthouse.

1855-1907, 11 volumes. Clerk's room, 4th floor.
1908—, 24 volumes. Clerk's office, south wall.

100. ACCRUED FEES
1921. 1 volume. (Discontinued).
Record of fees collected in civil and criminal cases showing date, amount, and from what source received. Alphabetically arranged. Handwritten on printed forms. 192 pages. 18 x 12 x 1.5. County courthouse. Clerk's office, east wall.

101. DEPOSITION REGISTER
1878-1879. 1 volume.
Record showing date, names who played up and defendant, name of case, and amount of fees. Alphabetically arranged. And written on printed forms. Condition poor. 315 pages. 18 x 8 x 1 County courthouse. Clerk's room, 4th floor, north wall.

102. FEE BOOK
1839-1908. 5 volumes.
Record of these received in the clerk's office showing date, from what source, and amount received. No index. And written on printed forms. Condition fair volumes average 250 pages. 14 x 11 x 1.5. County courthouse. Clerk's room, 4th floor, north wall.

103. WITNESS BLOTTER, CIVIL CASES
1886-1919. 10 volumes.
List of witnesses appearing in civil cases showing case number, names of plaintiff and defendant, date of appearance, and date fee was paid. Alphabetically arranged. Handwritten on printed forms. Volumes average 193 pages. 16 x 9 x 1. County courthouse. Clerk's room, 4th floor, east wall.

104. WITNESS BOOK, CIVIL CASES
1844-1930. 10 volumes (1-7, 10-12).
List of witnesses appearing in civil cases showing date, amount of fees collected, and names of cases. There is an apparent error in numbering of volumes, none missing. Alphabetically arranged. Handwritten on printed forms. Condition poor. Volumes average 414 pages. 18 x 8 x 1.5. County courthouse.
    1844-1919, 7 volumes. Clerk's room, 4th floor.
    1920-1930, 3 volumes. Clerk's office, east wall.

105. WITNESS BOOK, STATE CASES
1859—. 6 volumes. (1907-1919, missing).
List of witnesses appearing before the grand jury showing dates, names, and fees paid. Alphabetically arranged. Handwritten on printed forms. Condition fair. Volumes average 496 pages. 14 x 8 x 2. County courthouse.
    1859-1906, 4 volumes. Clerk's room, 4th floor, north wall.
    1905-1916, 2 volumes. Clerk's office, east wall.

106. WITNESS RECEIPT BOOK
1890-1916. 6 volumes.
Record of witnesses appearing in court showing their signatures for fees received, case numbers, and dates of appearances. Alphabetically arranged. And written on printed forms. Conditioned fair. Volumes average 198 pages. 16 x 8 x .5. County courthouse.
    1890-1904, 4 volumes. Clerk's room, 4th floor, north wall.
    1905-1916, 2 volumes. Clerk's office, east wall.

Bonds Posted

107. INJUNCTION BONDS
1920-1925. 1 file box. (15722-19103).
Copies of bonds posted in injunction suits showing names of plate of independent, date, amount of bond, and signature of clerk of courts. Numerically arranged. For index see entry 88. Handwritten and typed on printed forms. 8 x 12 x 4. County courthouse. Clerk's office, balcony, west wall.

108. MISCELLANEOUS BONDS
1910-1917. 1 file box.
Copies of bonds posted in various cases showing names of plaintiff and defendant, date, amount of bond, names of bondsman, and signature of clerk of courts. For index entry 88. Handwritten and typed on printed forms. 8 x 12 x 4. County courthouse. Clerk's office, balcony, west wall.

Motor Vehicle Records

109. BILLS OF SALE
1921—. 186 file boxes.
Duplicates of motor vehicle bills of sale showing name of grantor, date, vendor's license number, address, names of grantee and manufacturer, make of car, factory number, engine number, model, price, and signatures of grantor and grantee. Numerically arranged. For index see entry 110. Handwritten and typed on printed forms. File boxes 10 x 12 x 20 and 4 x 8 x 12. County courthouse.
1921-1930, 42 file boxes. Clerk's room, 4th floor.
1931—, 144 file boxes. Clerk's office, balcony, north wall.

110. INDEX TO MOTOR VEHICLE SALES
1921—. 14 volumes.
Alphabetical index of motor vehicle bills of sale and statements of ownership giving names of grantee and grand tour, date of filing, file number, amount of fee, and make and type of car. Handwritten on printed forms. Volumes average 500 pages (loose-leaf). County courthouse. Clerk's office, east wall.

Commissions and Licenses

111. APPOINTMENTS OF DEPUTY SHERIFFS
1915-1935. 3 volumes.
Record of deputies appointed by sheriff for regular and special duty showing name of each person, weather appointment is regular or special, date appointed or canceled, and signatures of sheriff and approving judge. Alphabetically arranged. Handwritten on printed forms. Volumes average 400 pages. 18 x 14 x 3. County courthouse. Clerk's office, east wall.

112. RECORD OF NOTARIES' COMMISSIONS
1858—. 12 volumes. (1-12).
Record of notaries commissioned by authority of governor showing name of governor granting commission, date, and oath of person appointed. Alphabetically arranged. Handwritten on printed forms. Condition fair. Volumes average 416

pages. 16 x 10 x 2. County courthouse.
>   1858-1891, 3 volumes. Clerk's room, 4^(th) floor.
>   1892—. 9 volumes. Clerk's office, balcony, east wall.

113. EMBALMERS' LICENSE RECORD
1902-1903. (1904-1908, missing). (Discontinued).
Record of licenses granted by state board of embalming examiners to persons practicing in county. After 1908 embalmers were required to register with board of health of village, city, or township in which they proposed to practice. Since 1917 they have been required to register with state board of health. Alphabetically arranged. Handwritten on printed forms. Condition fair. 280 pages. 10 x 16 x 1. County courthouse. Clerk's room, fourth floor, north wall.

114. OPTOMETRY RECORD
1920-1935. 1 volume.
Register of persons who were granted licenses by state board of optometry to practice in Trumbull County. Alphabetically arranged. Handwritten on printed forms. Condition poor. 104 pages. 16 x 8 x .5. County courthouse. Clerk's office, east wall.

115. RECORD OF RAILROAD POLICEMEN'S COMMISSIONS
1885—. 2 volumes.
Record of policemen commissioned by authority of governor to police railroad property showing name of governor making such an appointment, name of each appointee, date of appointment, and name of railroad company. Alphabetically arranged. Handwritten on printed forms. Volumes average 178 pages. 16 x 12 x 1.5. County courthouse. Clerk's office, east wall.

116. REGISTER OF REAL ESTATE LICENSES
1935—. 1 volume.
Record of licensed real estate dealers giving their names, addresses, and registration numbers. Alphabetically arranged. Handwritten on printed forms. 100 pages. 20 x 18 x 1. County courthouse. Clerk's office, east wall.

Naturalization Records

117. ALIEN DOCKET
1839-1847. 1 volume.
Record of foreign subjects making declarations of intentions of becoming naturalized citizens. See entry 133 for alien docket from 1848 to 1877. For index see entry 121. Handwritten. Condition fair. 200 pages. 12 x 6 x 1. County courthouse. Clerk's office, east wall.

118. NATURALIZATION PETITIONS
1907—. 26 volumes. (1-26).
Petition record of foreign-born persons for naturalization giving name of each person, age, nationality, date, address, and affidavits of petitioner and witnesses. See entries 197 and 198 for naturalization records before 1907. Since 1917 the county clerk of courts has had concurrent jurisdiction with the federal courts and citizenship matters. For index see entry 121. 1907-1921, handwritten on printed forms; 1922—, typed on printed forms. Condition fair. Volumes average 100 pages. 20 x 14 x 1. County courthouse. Clerk's office, east wall.

119. CITIZENSHIP PETITIONS GRANTED
1929—. 1 volume.
Petitions showing name of petitioner, date, and name of judge granting or refusing petition. Alphabetically arranged. Typed. 62 pages. 10 x 8 x .5. County courthouse. Clerk's office, east wall.

120. NATURALIZATION DIVISION (Departments of Commerce and Labor).
1907—. 17 volumes.
Record of declarations of intentions of foreign-born persons to become naturalized citizens giving name of person, address, date, nationality, and age. For index see entry 121. Handwritten and typed on U. S. Form 2202. Condition fair. 1 volume, 100 pages. 16 x 8 x .5; 16 volumes average 500 pages. 14 x 10 x 2. County courthouse. Clerk's office, east wall.

121. GENERAL INDEX TO NATURALIZATION
1906—. 1 volume.
Alphabetical index to naturalization records giving surname of person, given name, declaration of intention number. Petition number, and final certificate number. Handwritten on printed forms. 484 pages. 20 x 14 x 2. County courthouse. Clerk's office, east wall.

Coroner's Records

122. CORONER'S TRANSCRIPTS
1925—. 17 file boxes. (1980-4165).
Record of inquisitions made on deceased persons by county coroner. Numerically arranged. For index see entry 88. Typed on printed forms. 4 x 8 x 12. County courthouse. Clerk's office, west wall.

123. INQUEST RECORD
1883—. 2 volumes.
Record of inquests held by coroners and justices of peace giving date of each inquest, name a person, and name of officer holding inquest. Alphabetically arranged. Handwritten. Volumes average 400 pages. 20 x 14 x 2. County courthouse. Clerk's office, west wall.

Miscellaneous

124. ALIMONY RECORD
1928—. 1 volume.
Record of alimony payments kept for convenience of clerk of courts showing names of plaintiff and defendant, case number, amount of monthly payments, date, and check number. Alphabetically arranged. Handwritten on printed forms. 406 pages. 18 x 14 x 3.5. County courthouse. Clerk's office, counter.

125. RECORD OF FILES TAKEN FROM THE CLERK'S ROOM
1860-1878. 2 volumes.

Register of persons or attorneys taking records from clerk's office giving name of person, case number, date taken, and date returned. Alphabetically arranged. Handwritten on printed forms. Condition poor. 100 pages. 15 x 8 x 1. County courthouse. Clerk's room, 4th floor, north wall.

126. JUSTICES' OF PEACE OATHS
1861—. 4 volumes. (1-4).

Record of oaths sworn to by justices before clerk of courts giving date, name, and name of clerk swearing in the justice; also showing amount of bonds posted by justices. Alphabetically arranged. Handwritten on printed forms. Volumes average 358 pages. 16 x 8 x 1.5. County courthouse. Clerk's office, east wall.

127. MEMORIAL JOURNAL
1876-1928. 1 volume.

Record of resolutions drafted by bar committees when a member dies. Alphabetically arranged. Handwritten on printed forms. 464 pages. 18 x 12 x 2. County courthouse. Clerk's office, west wall.

128. ESTRAY BOOK
1815-1928. 3 volumes.

Record of strayed livestock giving date of each report, description of animal, and name a person who made report. No index. Handwritten. Condition for. Volumes 1815-1836 average 100 pages. 16 x 8 x .5; (1836-1928) Average 300 pages. 16 x 8 x 2. County courthouse.

 1815-1835, 2 volumes. Clerk's room, 4th floor, north wall.

 1836-1928, 1 volume. Clerk's office, east wall.

Jury Commission

129. Jury commissioners
1932—. 1 folder.
Copies of appointments and certified copies of the journal entry authorizing drawing of jury giving day, month, year, and number to be drawn; also names of judges, county clerk, and sheriff signing documents. No index. 8 x 14 x .125. Residence, Mrs. Nellie Elder, 690, Porter St., N.E., Warren, Ohio.

The judicial system for the territory comprising the present state of Ohio established a probate court. This court, established by an act of the Northwest Territory on August 30, 1788, consisted of a probate judge with jurisdiction in probate, testamentary, and guardianship matters, and two judges of the court of common pleas, who sat with him and ruled on contested points, defective sentences, and final judgments. (Pease, *op. cit.,* 9).

The judicial system established in 1803, under the first constitution of Ohio, made no provision for a probate court but invested such powers as had been exercised by the court in the territorial period in the court of common pleas. The constitution of 1851 recreated the probate court and gave it original jurisdiction of all probate and testamentary matters, and the appointment and supervision of guardians, and such other jurisdiction that might be provided by law. (*Ohio Const. 1851* Art. IV, sec. 8). An amendment in 1912 authorized the common pleas judge, when petitioned by ten percent of the qualified voters in the counties having a population less than sixty thousand, to submit the question of combining the probate court and the court of common pleas to the voters at any general election. (*Ohio Const.,* Art. IV, sec. 7).

One of the primary functions of the court since its inception has been the settlement of estates. By the civil code adopted in 1853, the court was given original jurisdiction in taking proof of wills, in granting letters testamentary, and in settling accounts of executors and administrators. (51 O. L. 167). Until 1854 the court had jurisdiction in the matters of enforcing the payment of debts and legacies of deceased persons. While the court retains the original jurisdiction regarding estates, new duties have been added in recent years. With the development of inheritance tax laws as a new means of taxation the probate court has been required to determine and assess the tax after the county auditor has appraised the decedent's estate. (108 O. L. pt. I, 561).

By constitutional provision the probate court has original jurisdiction in granting marriage licenses and licenses to ministers to solemnize marriages. The former provision was modified by an act adopted in 1931, which requires an elapse of at least five days between the time of application and the issuance of marriage licenses. (114 O. L. 93). Moreover, the probate courts in certain counties were given concurrent jurisdictions with the court of common pleas in "divorce, foreclosure, and partition cases." Thus, in 1894, the legislature conferred such jurisdiction upon the probate courts in Allen, Richland, Perry, Defiance, and Wood counties. (91 O. L. 799-800).

The original act, subject to amendment in 1896, 1900, and 1904, which granted and denied such jurisdiction to the probate courts in certain counties, was repealed in 1911. (92 O. L. 643; 94 O. L. 137-138; 97 O. L. 113-114; 102 O. L. 100). In 1919 concurrent jurisdiction was re-established in Pickaway, Licking, Perry, Defiance, Henry, and Ashland Counties, and established in Fayette County. (108 O. L. pt. 1, 625). This jurisdiction was abolished in 1931. (114 O. L. 320).

The jurisdiction of the court extends to the state's unfortunates. The constitution of 1851 gave the court jurisdiction in making inquests respecting lunatics, insane persons, and idiots. The constitutional provision in this respect was interrupted by the civil code of 1853. Since 1855 the court has been given jurisdiction in the appointment of guardians for minors, idiots, imbeciles, lunatics, and other incompetents by reason of advanced age. A year later, the court was authorized to commit persons who were mentally incompetent to state institutions maintained for such purposes. (53 O. L. 81). In recent years the court has been given jurisdiction in trial cases involving neglected, dependent, and delinquent children. (See juvenile court). In certain counties, however, this jurisdiction has been transferred to the newly established courts of domestic relations.

During the early years of its existence the court was given limited criminal jurisdiction in cases in which the sentence did not impose capital punishment or punishment by imprisonment. By the code of civil procedure (1853) the judgments and final decrees of the probate court could be reviewed by the court of common pleas on error. (51 O. L. 146). In 1857 the criminal jurisdiction of the probate court was transferred to the court of common pleas (54 O. L. 97) but later acts retain it in certain counties only. The last vestige of criminal jurisdiction disappeared with the adoption of the probate code in 1931. (114 O. L. 475).

Miscellaneous duties, remotely related to probate and testamentary matters, have been added by legislative action. Since 1888 the court has been required to file a certified list of all unknown depositors as furnished by the institutions or persons engaged in loaning money for profit. (85 O. L. 65). The present duty of changing the names of persons who desire it had its beginning in 1898. (92 O. L. 21). Since 1908 the probate court has been required to file certificates of doctors and surgeons, and since 1916 the certificates of registered nurses which authorize them to practice their professions in the county. (99 O. L. 499; 106 O. L. 193). Since 1913 the court has been invested with the power to grant injunctions (103 O. L. 427), and since 1915 has had concurrent jurisdiction with the court of common pleas in condemnation proceedings for roads. (105 O. L. 583).

The probate judge, aside from his authority to appoint guardians and administrators, has enjoyed an additional appointee power which was conferred upon him by a legislative act of 1861. Under the provisions of this act he was, and is, authorized to appoint one gager and inspector of spirits, linseed, lard, and coal oil; one inspector of flour and meal; one inspector of beef, pork, lard, and butter; one inspector of sawyer lumber and shingles; and one inspector of salt. (58 O. L. 105). Since 1913 he has had authority to appoint members of the county board of visitors (which see), and since 1917 the city boards of park commissioners. (103 O. L. 173-174, 88; 137 O. L. 65).

The probate judge, like other county officials, has been required by statute to keep a record of the business of his office. The present system of records, originating for the most part in 1853 and continued by the probate code of 1931, includes a criminal record, administrative docket, guardian's docket, marriage record, record of bonds, naturalization record, and a permanent record of births and deaths. (51 O. L. 167; 52 O. L. 103; 75 O. L. 9; 114 O. L. 324).

The probate judge has the care and custody of the files, papers, books, and records belonging to the probate office. The probate code, adopted in 1931, directed the probate judge to preserve for future reference and examination of all pleadings, accounts, vouchers, and other papers in each estate, trust, assignment, and guardianship, or other proceedings. Such papers are to be properly jacketed and tied together. Moreover, he is required to make proper entries and indexes omitted by his predecessor. Certificates of marriages, reports of birth, and similar papers not a part of a case or proceeding are to be arranged and preserved separately in the order of dates in which they are filed. (114 O. L. 321-322).

At present the probate judge is elected for a four-year term. (114 O. L. 320). In recent years there has been an attempt to raise the qualifications of those seeking election to this office. Accordingly, in 1935 the probate code of 1931 was amended and eligibility to the office was restricted to a practicing attorney or to a person who "*shall have previously served as a probate judge immediately prior to his election.*" (116 O. L. 481).

Juvenile Court

The juvenile court, though of uncertain origin, has been gradually recognized as an American contribution to the administration of social justice. The establishment of such courts was the logical outcome of the practical philosophy of enlightened public men that child offenders against the law, or conventional social standards, shall not be treated as criminals, but as unfortunate needing the help, supervision, and protection of the state. (Miriam Van Waters, *Youth in Conflict,* New York, 1925, 147, 159, 161). Although the idea of a separate court for the trial of juvenile offenders was an institution of gradual growth, the first court of this kind in the United States was established in 1899, in Chicago, Cook County, Illinois, by an act of the legislature of that state. The Illinois experiment gave an impetus to the children's movement in the middle west. (Edwin H. Sutherland, *Principles of Criminology,* Chicago 1934, 270-272).

The Ohio legislature was not slow in seeing the advantage of the Illinois experiment, and accordingly, in 1902, an act was passed creating the juvenile court in Cuyahoga County. Under this act all counties having a population of over 380,000 and an insolvency court was authorized, under an extension of the jurisdiction of this court, to establish children's courts. It gave the court jurisdiction of the trial of cases involving delinquent and neglected children; defined the terms "delinquent, dependent, and neglected;" authorized the appointment of a probation officer, and made it his duty to investigate the facts by cases coming before the court, and to take charge of the offender before and after the trial. The clerk of the juvenile court was directed to keep a journal in which was to be recorded the minutes of the case. The judge was to serve for a period of five years, (95 O. L. 785). The term remained at five years until 1935 when it was extended to six years.

Two years after the establishment of the Cuyahoga County juvenile court, the assembly provided, by statute, for the establishment of juvenile courts in the rural counties of the state which, because of their lack of population, was unable to create the newer agencies under the provisions of the act of 1902. Under the act of 1904 the judges of the court of common pleas, probate court, and where established, the insolvency courts, wherein three or more judges held court concurrently, were authorized to appoint one of their members as "juvenile judge." The court was given original jurisdiction in all cases involving neglected, dependent and delinquent children under the age of sixteen years; and all children, who, in the past, had been scheduled for trial in a justice of the peace or police court were in the future to be tried before a juvenile judge. As under the act of 1902, the judge was authorized to appoint a probation officer, and the clerk of courts was directed to keep a journal of the minutes in each case. (97 O. L. 561). In 1908 the court was given jurisdiction in cases involving minors under seventeen years of age, and, such children as were brought before the juvenile judge were to become wards of the court until they had attained the age of twenty-one years. Moreover, the county commissioners were authorized to provide by lease or purchase a "detention home" where neglected or dependent children might be detained pending the final disposition of their cases. The clerk of courts was directed to keep not only a journal, but also an appearance docket containing all orders, judgments, and findings of the court. It provided, also, for case studies to be made by the probation officer. (99 O. L. 196). The age jurisdiction of the court was increased to eighteen in 1913. (103 O. L. 877).

Marked progress has been made in the medical treatment of juveniles. While the act of 1913 authorized the juvenile judge to submit any child sentenced to an institution for correction to a mental test, the act of 1929 authorized him to submit any child coming before the court to a mental and physical test to be made by a physician or psychiatrist. (103 O. L. 872; 113 O. L. 471). To further the scientific handling of children, the county commissioners were authorized, in the same year, to lease or construct a separate building to be known as the "juvenile court" which should be appropriately constructed, arranged, furnished and maintained for the convenience and effective transaction of the business of the court, including adequate facilities to be used as laboratories, dispensaries, or clinics with the scientific use of specialist attached to the court. (113 O. L. 470).

One of the guiding principles of the court has been to make its "custody and discipline" of children approximate as nearly as possible that which should be given by their parents. In the case involving neglected or dependent children, not sentenced to state institutions, it has been the policy of judges to assign children to private homes, and make arrangements for their adoption. Many other functions have been taken over by the juvenile court such as mothers' pensions. (103 O. L. 877).

The juvenile court of Cuyahoga County is the only independent juvenile court in the state. There are seven other juvenile courts in Ohio, all attached to the court of domestic relations. (See court of domestic relations). In smaller counties the probate judge is assigned all juvenile cases.

Calendars and Dockets

130. PROBATE COURT CALENDAR
1882——. 58 volumes.

Records of cases to be tried in probate court showing date, case number, name of attorney, and disposition of case. Chronologically arranged. Handwritten. Condition fair. Volumes average 130 pages. 14 x 10 x .5. County courthouse.

    1881-1927, 42 volumes. Probate court storage, attic
    1928——, 16 volumes. Probate court office under counter.

131. SETTLEMENT CALENDAR
1879-1909. 3 volumes.

Record of settlements of guardians and administrators giving names of descendants and wards; also their address and accounts. Alphabetically arranged. Handwritten. Condition poor. Volumes average 234 pages. 18 x 14 x 1. County courthouse. Probate court storage, attic, south of elevator.

132. ADMINISTRATION DOCKET
1877——. 28 volumes. (11-38).

Record of appraisers appointed and appraisements filed; also administrators applications, statements, and affidavits. Some of early records were destroyed in courthouse fire of 1895. Alphabetically arranged. For index see entry 137. Handwritten. Condition fair. Volumes average 540 pages. 16 x 10 x 2. County courthouse. Probate court office, south wall.

133. ALIEN DOCKET
1848-1877. 1 volume.

Naturalization records showing names of foreign born persons appearing for naturalization, age, place of birth, residence, and nationality. See entries 197 and 198 for naturalization records from 1859 to 1906 and entries 117-121 for naturalization records after 1906. Since 1917 the county clerk of courts has concurrent jurisdiction with the federal courts in citizenship matters. Alphabetically arranged. For index see entry 137. Handwritten. Volumes average 352 pages. 16 x 8 x 1. County courthouse. Probate court office, west wall.

134. ASSIGNMENT DOCKET
1861—. 2 volumes.
Record of deeds of assignment showing names of assignees, assignors' claims, and reports of public sales filed and approved by the court. Alphabetically arranged. For index see entry 137. Handwritten. Volumes average 320 pages. 18 x 12 x 1. County courthouse. Probate court office, north wall.

135. CIVIL DOCKET
1852—. 17 volumes. (1-17).
Records of proceedings of civil cases in probate court. Alphabetically arranged. For index see entry 137. Handwritten. Volumes average 500 pages. 16 x 10 x 2. County courthouse. Probate court office, west wall.

136. GUARDIAN DOCKET
1882—. 7 volumes. (1-7).
Docket of guardianship cases giving name of case and date. Also applications filed for appointments of guardians and hearings ordered and notices issued. Alphabetically arranged. For index see entry 137. Handwritten. Volumes average 500 pages. 16 x 8 x 2.25. County courthouse. Probate court office, north wall.

137. GENERAL INDEX TO ESTATES
n. d. 2 volumes.
Alphabetical index to estate records giving case number, name of estate, ward, assignor, etc; also to administration, civil, guardians', and assignees' dockets giving volume and page numbers and remarks. Handwritten and typed on printed forms. Volumes average 554 pages. 20 x 14 x 2.5. County courthouse. Probate court office on counter.

138. PRAECIPE DOCKET
1850-1902. 1 volume.
Calendar of cases heard in probate court: also list of attorneys who heard these cases involving equity. No index. Handwritten. Conditioned poor. Volumes average 300 pages. 14 x 8 x 1. County courthouse. Probate court storage, attic, south of elevator.

Record of Trials

139. QUARTER SESSIONS RECORD
1800-1828. 1 volume.

This is the oldest and most valuable official county record of Trumbull County, and contains a record of first civil officers, court and marriage records, court orders, petitions for roads, record of licenses to operate taverns and places of public entertainment, appointments of justices of the peace, appointments of committees to lay out various townships, roads, jail, and all other public matters including surveys in early history of the Western Reserve. Chronologically arranged. Handwritten. Condition poor. 351 pages. 16 x 12 x 2. County courthouse. Probate court office, balcony, west wall.

140. JOURNAL
1852—. 108 volumes. (1-108).

Records and journal entries of probate court proceedings. Alphabetically arranged. 1852-1917, handwritten; 1918—, typed. Volumes average 500 pages. 18 x 12 x 2.25. County courthouse. Probate court office, south and west walls.

141. CIVIL CASES
1862-1931. 69 file boxes. (1-4270).

Miscellaneous civil cases such as epileptic cases, petitions for determination of inheritance, settlements of various cases, and disposition of cases. Numerically arranged. Handwritten and typed. 8 x 4 x 12. , County courthouse. Probate court office, east wall.

142. CRIMINAL RECORD
1853-1931. 6 volumes. (1-6) (Discontinued).

Record of affidavits and journal entries of criminal cases in probate court. Alphabetically arranged. Handwritten. Volumes average 500 pages. 20 x 12 x 2. County courthouse.

1853-1903, 2 volumes. Probate court storage, attic.
1904-1931, 4 volumes. Probate court office, south wall.

143. HABEAS CORPUS
1853-1869. 1 volume.

Record of *habeas corpus* proceedings of probate court cases. Alphabetically arranged. Handwritten, Condition fair. 480 pages. 16 x 10 x 1.5. County courthouse. Probate court storage, attic, south of elevator.

144. INSOLVENCY CASES
1855-1922. 2 volumes.

Record of applications for certificates of insolvency; affidavits and petitions filed in insolvency cases are included in this record. No index. Handwritten. Condition poor. Volumes average 200 pages. 14 x 6 x 1. County courthouse. Probate court office, west wall.

145. ASSIGNMENTS
1862—. 31 file boxes. (1-330).

Assignment and disposition records of real and personal property cases filed in probate court. Numerically arranged. Handwritten and typed. 8 x 4 x 12. County courthouse. Probate court office, east wall.

146. RAILROAD APPROPRIATION
1833-1919. 4 volumes. (1-4).

Record of petitions for the appropriation of private property for railroad right of ways. Petitions reviewed and cases tried in court, verdicts and agreements reached. Record gives location of property in question, name of railroad company, and date of filing and settlement. Alphabetically indexed. 1833-1912, handwritten; 1912-1919 typed. Volumes average 350 pages. 16 x 10 x 1.25. County courthouse. Probate court office, west wall.

147. RECORD OF PRIVATE SALE OF PERSONAL PROPERTY
1928—. 2 volumes. (2-3) (Volume No. 1 prior to 1928, missing).

Petition record to sell personal property at private sale giving description and appraised value of such property. Alphabetically arranged. Typed. Volumes average 500 pages. 20 x 12 x 2. County courthouse.

    1928-1934, 1 volume. Probate court storage, attic, south of elevator.

    1934—, 1 volume. Probate court office, west wall.

Official Bonds and Bonds and Letters of Fiduciaries

148. LIQUOR DEALERS' BONDS
1882. 1 volume.

Record of bonds to engage in sale of intoxicating liquor giving name of property owner, description of property, amount of bond, and date. Alphabetically arranged. Handwritten. 321 pages. 14 x 8 x 1. County courthouse. Probate court storage, addict, south of elevator.

149. OFFICERS' MISCELLANEOUS BONDS
1821—. 5 volumes. (1-5).

Record of miscellaneous bonds approved by probate court including those for testamentary trustees, letters of authority, and additional guardian bonds. Alphabetically arranged. Handwritten on printed forms. Condition fair. Volumes average 475 pages. 15 x 10 x 2. County courthouse.

> 1821-1926, 4 volumes. Probate court storage, attic.
> 1927—, 1 volume. Probate court office, west wall.

150. ADMINISTRATORS' BONDS AND LETTERS
1868-1913. 6 volumes. (2-7) (Discontinued).

Letters of appointments; also bonds fixed by probate court. Alphabetically arranged. Handwritten. Volumes average 612 pages. 16 x 12 x 2. County courthouse. Probate court storage, attic, south of elevator.

151. ADMINISTRATORS' BONDS AND LETTERS (Wills Annexed)
1880-1931. 3 volumes. (13-).

Record of administrators' bonds and probate court appointments. Alphabetically arranged. 1880-1927, handwritten; 1928-1931, typed. Volumes average 610 pages. 16 x 10 x 2. County courthouse. Probate court storage, attic, south of elevator.

152. ADMINISTRATORS DE BONIS NON AND DE BONIS NON WITH ANNEXED
1926-1931. 2 volumes. (Discontinued).

Record of administrators appointments, bonds fixed, and letters of authority by probate court showing date, amount of bond, and in what matters. Alphabetically arranged. Typed. Volumes average 600 pages. 20 x 10 x 3. County courthouse. Probate court storage, attic, south of elevator.

153. ADMINISTRATORS', EXECUTORS ADDITIONAL BONDS
1882-1919. 1 volume.
Record of petitions filed asking for an order to sell real estate giving description of property. In some cases after reviewing said petition the court increased the bond of administrator or executor. Alphabetically arranged. Handwritten. Condition fair. 380 pages. 14 x 8 x 1. County courthouse. Probate court storage, attic, south of elevator.

154. GUARDIANS' BONDS AND LETTERS
1853—. 12 volumes. (1-11, 2 volumes No.2).
Record of appointments and letters of authority by probate court. Alphabetically indexed. 1853-1931, handwritten; 1932—, typed. Volumes average 482 pages. 16 x 10 x 2.5. County courthouse.
    1853-1931, 10 volumes. Probate court storage, attic.
    1932—. 2 volumes. Probate court office, west wall.

155. GUARDIANS' ADDITIONAL BONDS
1882-1921. 1 volume. (Discontinued).
Record of guardians appointed by probate court and of their bonds fixed; also petitions to the court to sell real estate and of the appointment of appraisers. Alphabetically indexed. Handwritten on printed forms. 375 pages. 12 x 8 x 1. County courthouse. Probate court storage, attic, south of elevator.

156. EXECUTORS' BONDS AND LETTERS
1888—. 11 volumes. (2-12).
Record of bonds and letters of authority by probate court. Alphabetically arranged. 1888-1929, handwritten on printed forms; 1930—, typed. Condition fair. Volumes average 540 pages. 16 x 10 x 2. County courthouse.
    1888-1931, 8 volumes. Probate court storage, attic.
    1932—. 3 volumes. Probate court office, west wall.

157. RESIDUARY LEGATEES' BONDS
1883-1911. 1 volume.

Record of bonds fixed by probate court in the matters of residuary legatees showing amount, date, and in what matter. See entry 149 for residuary legatees' bond record after 1911. Alphabetically arranged. Handwritten on printed forms. 460 pages. 14 x 8 x 2. County courthouse. Probate court storage, attic, south of elevator.

158. TRUSTEE BONDS
1884-1906. 1 volume.

Record of appointments of trustees and their bonds as fixed by the court; also their oaths, duties, and date. Alphabetically arranged. Handwritten. 460 pages. 14 x 8 x 2. County courthouse. Probate court office, west wall.

Settlement of Estates

159. APPLICATIONS FOR LETTERS OF ADMINISTRATION
1913—. 14 volumes. (8-21).

Statements and applications for appointment of appraisers together with court orders of appointments and letters of authority issued by probate court. Alphabetically arranged. 1913 1921, handwritten; 1931—, typed. Volumes average 600 pages. 18 x 12 x 2. County courthouse. Probate court office, west wall.

160. NOTICE RECORD
1886—. 10 volumes. (1-10).

Record of trustees, guardians, and administrators appointed by probate court and proofs of publication sworn before notaries. Alphabetically arranged. Handwritten on printed forms. Volumes average 475 pages. 18 x 12 x 2. County courthouse.

    1886-1932, 9 volumes. Probate court storage, attic.

    1933—, 1 volume. Probate court office, west wall.

161. SCHEDULE OF CLAIMS, DEBTS, AND LIABILITIES
1932—. 4 volumes.

Administrators' reports to probate court of all claims, debts, and liabilities; also court orders amending approvements of debts. Alphabetically arranged. Typed. Volumes average 500 pages. 18 x 10 x 2.25. County courthouse. Probate court office, west wall.

162. ESTATES RELEASED FROM ADMINISTRATION
1918—. 1 volume.
Record of applications to release an estate from administrator and directing all payments and delivery to proper person. Alphabetically arranged. Typed. 500 pages. 18 x 12 x 2. County courthouse, probate court office, west wall.

163. ASSIGNEE RECORD
1860-1929. 12 volumes. (1-12).
Record of re-assignments, inventories, and appraisements of estates; record of court proceedings, itemized inventories, court orders for sales and assignments; also deeds for creditor assignments. Alphabetically arranged. Handwritten. Volumes average 600 pages. 18 x 12 x 3. County courthouse. Probate court office, west wall.

164. GUARDIANSHIPS
1882—. 219 file boxes.
Guardianship papers, settlements of estates, inventory and appraisement records. Numerically arranged. Handwritten and typed. 8 x 4 x 12. County courthouse. Probate court office, east wall.

165. GUARDIAN'S INVENTORY
1877—. 3 volumes. (1-3).
Record of guardians' inventory of estates showing property values and rentals derived. Alphabetically arranged. 1877-1924, handwritten; 1924—, typed. Volumes average 612 pages. 18 x 12 x 3. County courthouse.
1877-1924, 1 volume. Probate court storage, attic.
1925—, 2 volumes. Probate court office, west wall.

166. INVENTORY AND SALE BILL
1876—. 74 volumes. (9-82) (Prior to 1876 destroyed by courthouse fire of 1895).
Record of appraisers appointed and their oaths; also record of their inventories of real and personal property. Alphabetically arranged. 1876-1920, handwritten; 1921—, typed. Volumes average 612 pages. 20 x 12 x 2. County courthouse.
1876-1933, 65 volumes. Probate court storage, attic.
1934—, 9 of volumes. Probate court office, west wall.

167. FINAL RECORD OF ACCOUNTS
1853—. 53 volumes.

Detailed and complete record of accounts in guardianship cases filed in probate court. Alphabetically arranged. 1853-1908, handwritten; 1909—, typed. Condition fair. Volumes average 638 pages. 20 x 12 x 2. County courthouse.

    1853-1934, 52 volumes. Probate court storage, attic.

    1935—, 2 volumes. Probate court office, west wall.

168. FINAL RECEIPTS
1881—. 6 volumes. (1-6).

Final receipt record of guardians, executors, and administrators in settlement of estates. Alphabetically arranged. 1881-1911, handwritten; 1912—, typed. Volumes average 700 pages. 14 x 10 x 3. County courthouse.

    1881-1926, 2 volumes. Probate court storage, attic.

    1927—, 4 volumes. Probate court office, west wall.

169. ESTATES
1805—. 416 file boxes.

Copies of wills, settlement papers, and proofs of publications; also court records of appointments of administrators, executors, and guardians. Numerically arranged. For index see entry 137. Handwritten and typed. 12 x 12 x 22 and 8 x 4 x 12. County courthouse.

    1805-1912, 72 file boxes. Probate court storage, attic.

    1913—, 344 file boxes. Probate court office, east and north and south walls.

170. ESTATES
n. d. 15 cardboard boxes, 2 wooden boxes.

Copies of wills, settlement of estate records, and proof of publications. The boxes are closed and show no legible markings to indicate indexing. Sizes varies from 10 x 8 x 12 to 14 x 18 x 24. County courthouse. Probate court storage, attic.

171. DISTRIBUTION OF ASSETS

1925-1935. 3 volumes. (1-3).

Petition record for distribution of assets and journal entries of approval of the court; also assets and agreements of distributors when all debts of estates are paid. Alphabetically arranged. Typed. Volumes average 500 pages. 18 x 10 x 2. County courthouse.

1925-1928, 1 volume. Probate court storage, attic.

1929—, 2 volumes. Probate court office, west wall.

172. WILL RECORD

1841—, 57 volumes. (1-57).

Record of applications to probate wills showing witnesses' testimonies and copies of wills. Alphabetically arranged. 1841-1925, handwritten; 1925—, typed. Volumes average 516 pages. 20 x 14 x 2.25. County courthouse. Probate court office, south and west walls.

173. ELECTION OF WIDOW OR WIDOWER

1905—. 2 volumes.

Elections and appointments of widows or widowers in probate court. Alphabetically arranged. Handwritten. Volumes average 453 pages. 8 x 12 x 2.5. County courthouse. Probate court office, west wall.

174. INHERITANCE TAX

1898-1935. 5 volumes.

Record of estates inherited showing value of real and personal property constituting such estates and the amount of indebtedness against it; also the amount of tax fixed by court. Alphabetically arranged. 1898-1914, handwritten; 1915-1935, typed. Volumes average 500 pages. 20 x 14 x 2.5. County courthouse.

1898-1928, 4 volumes. Probate court storage, attic.

1929-1935, 1 volume. Probate court office, west wall.

175. PETITION RECORD

1856—. 64 volumes.

Record of guardians' applications for various allowances and to correct the inventory and appraisement of estates in the determination of inheritance taxes; also briefs filed for the modification of inheritance taxes. Alphabetically arranged.

Handwritten and typed. Volumes average 500 pages. 20 x 12 x 2.5. County courthouse. Probate court office, south wall.

Record of Dependents

176. E. RECORD (Indentures)
1824-1869. 1 volume.
Record of indentures between various parties for the purpose of "binding out" minors as apprentices showing the name of all parties concerned, age of minor, length of time for which bound, and all considerations entering into the contract. No index. Handwritten. Condition poor. 300 pages. 18 x 12 x 1.25. County courthouse. Probate court storage, attic.

177. ADOPTION RECORD
1904—. 5 volumes. (1-5).
Record of petitions for the adoption of minor children; also answers, consents, and court orders regarding the petitions. Alphabetically arranged. 1904-1921, handwritten; 1922—, typed. Volumes average 480 pages. 18 x 12 x 2. County courthouse. Probate court office, south wall.

178. EPILEPSY, FINAL RECORD
1879—. 2 volumes.
Record of applications for admission into state institution for epileptics; also medical certificates and examiners' inquest in the case, transcripts, findings, and court orders. It also shows date of application, hearing, examination, final court order, and date and signature of examining physicians. Records of feeble-minded youths are included. See entry 179 for records of feeble-minded before 1929. Alphabetically arranged. 1897-1929, handwritten on printed forms; 1930—, typed on printed forms. Volumes average 600 pages. 18 x 12 x 2. County courthouse. Probate court office, west wall.

179. FEEBLE-MINDED (Youth Record)
1905-1929. 1 volume.
Record of applications for admission of feeble-minded youths sent to Ohio State Hospital; of persons admitted and copies of medical examinations. It shows date, full name, address, age, and name of examining physician. Alphabetically arranged.

Handwritten on printed forms. 150 pages. 18 x 14 x 1.5. County courthouse. Probate court office, west wall.

180. LUNACY RECORD
1864—. 12 volumes. (1-12).
Final records of inquests of lunacy showing statements of medical witnesses; certificates are included. Alphabetically arranged. Handwritten. Volumes average 402 pages. 18 x 12 x 1.75. County courthouse. Probate court office, south wall.

Juvenile Cases

181. MOTHERS' PENSION DOCKET
1914—. 5 volumes. (I-5).
Record of pension cases considered in probate court and of monthly amounts allowed by the court. Alphabetically arranged. Handwritten. Volumes average 320 pages. 16 x 12 x 2. County courthouse. Probate court office, Juvenile Department, south wall.

182. MOTHERS' PENSION RECORDS
1892-1934, 6 volumes.
Record of applications filed at juvenile court for allowances of support. Alphabetically arranged. Typed. Volumes average 592 pages. 20 x 10 x 3. County courthouse.
1892-1934, 4 volumes. Probate court office, Juvenile Department, south wall.
1927-1932, 2 volumes. Probate court storage, attic, south of elevator.

183. MOTHERS' PENSIONS
1914—. 27 file boxes. (1-1280).
Juvenile court records of orders discontinuing allowances to mothers who now have other sources of income. Numerically arranged. Handwritten and typed. 8 x 4 x 12. County courthouse. Probate court office, east wall.

184. JUVENILE COURT DOCKET
1934—. 1 volume.
Record of cases referred to probate court from court of common pleas regarding

care and custody of children showing amounts of money received from defendants and paid to plaintiffs for support of minors. Alphabetically arranged. Handwritten. 500 pages. 14 x 12 x 2. County courthouse. Probate court office, Juvenile Department, south wall.

185. JUVENILE DOCKET
1934—. 10 volumes. (1-10).
Record of juvenile cases such as delinquents and minors who have been committed to institutions. Alphabetically arranged. Handwritten on printed forms. Volumes average 500 pages. 16 x 12 x 2.5. County courthouse. Probate court office, Juvenile Department, south wall.

186. JUVENILE CASES
1915—. 57 file boxes. (1-4000).
Record of cases where minor children are brought before probate court and of disposition of these cases. Numerically arranged. Handwritten and typed. 8 x 4 x 12. County courthouse. Probate court office, east wall.

187. JUVENILE COURT ADULT CASES
1934—. 1 volume.
Record of petitions filed and decisions in non-support and delinquency cases regarding support of minors. Alphabetically arranged. Handwritten. 500 pages. 16 x 12 x 2.5 County courthouse. Probate court office, Juvenile Department, south wall.

188. ADULT CASES
1934—. 3 file boxes. (1-219).
Court records of non-support cases; citations and judgments for support of minor children. Numerically arranged. Handwritten and typed. 12 x 8 x 4. County courthouse. Probate court office, east wall.

Vital Statistics

189. BIRTH RECORDS
1867-1908. 4 volumes. (1-4) (After 1908 kept by state board of health).
Birth registrations in probate court showing date, names the parents, place of residence, and race. Alphabetically arranged. Handwritten on printed forms. Average 300 pages. 20 x 12 x 3. County courthouse. Probate court office, balcony, west wall.

190. DEATH RECORD
1867-1908. 3 volumes. (1-3) (After 1908 kept by state board of health).
List of deaths recorded in probate court office giving full name, date, age, place of birth, residence at time of death, and occupation st time of death. Alphabetically arranged. Handwritten on printed forms. Volume average 320 pages. 18 x 12 x 2. County courthouse. Probate court office, south wall.

191. WRONGFUL DEATH SETTLEMENT
1927—. 1 volume.
Applications for consent of the court in settlement actions for damages by wrongful death; also journal entries of such actions. Alphabetically indexed. Typed. 500 pages. 20 x 12 x 2. County courthouse. Probate court office, west wall.

192. MARRIAGE RECORD
1816-1891. 18 volumes.
Record of personal appearances in probate court of persons seeking marriage licenses. Alphabetically arranged. Handwritten on printed forms. Volumes, (1816-1842) average 240 pages 12 x 8 x 2; (1843-1891) 688 pages 14 x 8 x 2. County courthouse. Probate court office, north wall.

193. MARRIAGE CERTIFICATES
1843—. 14 file boxes.
Certificates of marriages showing date, place of marriage, and official or minister officiating. 1883-1902, chronologically arranged; 1903—, numerically arranged. Handwritten and typed on printed forms. 8 x 14 x 12. County courthouse. Probate court office, east wall.

194. MARRIAGE RECORD
1828—. 31 volumes. (2-32).

Record of marriage licenses issued by probate court showing name of contracting parties, dates, ages, and name of official or minister who performed ceremony. See entry 139 for marriage records before 1828. Alphabetically arranged. Handwritten and handwritten on printed forms. Volumes average 650 pages. 20 x 12 x 3. County courthouse. Probate court office, north and south walls.

Licenses

195. RELIGIOUS SOCIETIES - MINISTERS OF THE GOSPEL
1820-1871. 1 volume.

Record of church and religious organizations showing when organized and incorporated, dates, and locations; also register of ordained ministers authorized to perform marriages in state of Ohio. Alphabetically arranged. Handwritten. 111 pages. 14 x 8 x 1. County courthouse. Probate court office, west wall.

196. MINISTERS' LICENSES
1871-1921. 2 volumes.

Record of ministers licenses to preach and solemnize marriages in Trumbull County showing where license was first granted, full name, address, denomination, and date. Alphabetically indexed by names. Handwritten on printed forms. Volumes average 452 pages. 14 x 8 x 2. County courthouse. Probate court office, west wall.

197 LIMITED PRACTITIONERS, RECORD OF REGISTERED NURSES
1916—. 1 volume.

Record of graduate nurses and certificates issued to nurses; also record of limited practitioners and certificates of authority granted by state to practice showing name, address, and date of certificate. Alphabetically arranged. Handwritten on printed forms. 204 pages. 16 x 10 x 1. County courthouse. Probate court office, west wall.

Naturalization Records

198. CERTIFICATES Of NATURALIZATION
1859-1906. 7 volumes. (1-6, 2 volumes No. 2).
Certificates of foreign- born subjects who became naturalized citizens showing date, nationality, place of birth, place of arrival in United States, and date of naturalization. See entry 133 for alien docket, 1848-1877; see entries 117-121 for naturalization records after 1906. Alphabetically arranged. Handwritten on printed forms. Volumes average 642 pages. 12 x 8 x 2.5. County courthouse. Probate court office, west wall.

199. NATURALIZATION RECORD, MINORS
1861-1906. 6 volumes. (1-6).
Declarations of aliens arriving in United States before reaching age of 19 years and showing place of birth, nationality, and date of declaration. These contain final probate court records of naturalization. Alphabetically arranged. Handwritten on printed forms. Volumes average 610 pages. 14 x 8 x 2.75. County courthouse. Probate court office, west wall.

Fiscal Accounts

200. CASH BOOK
1885—. 18 volumes.
Record of all money received in probate court office giving date, name of payee, and purpose; also list of witnesses and jurors and amount of fees. No index. Handwritten on printed forms. Conditioned poor. Volumes average 424 pages. 18 x 8 x 2. County courthouse.
    1885-1914, 2 volumes. Probate court storage, attic.
    1915—, 16 volumes. Probate court office, north wall.

201. COST BILL
1882-1904. 10 volumes (Discontinued).
Itemized record of court costs in appointment of executors and administrators. Alphabetically arranged. Handwritten. Condition fair. Volumes average 320 pages. 14 x 8 x 1. County courthouse. Probate court storage, attic.

202. COST BILL RECORD
1886-1909. 4 volumes.
Record of petitions for sale of real estate. Discontinued soon after county office was taken from fee bases(98 O. L. 94, 173). Alphabetically arranged. Condition fair. Volumes average 320 pages. 14 x 8 x 1. County courthouse. Probate court storage, attic, south of elevator.

203. COST BILL RECORD OF ACCOUNTS
1888-1890. 2 volumes. (Discontinued).
Itemized record of court costs in matter of final accounts. Alphabetically arranged. Handwritten on printed forms. Volumes average 298 pages. 14 x 8 x 1. County courthouse. Probate court storage, attic.

204. COST BILL, GUARDIANS
1992-1901. 2 volumes. (Discontinued).
Itemized record of court cost in appointment of guardians. Alphabetically arranged. Handwritten on printed forms. Condition fair. Volumes average 320 pages. 16 x 8 x 1. County courthouse. Probate court storage, attic.

205. COST BILL
1885-1899. 1 volume. (Discontinued).
Itemized record of court costs in criminal cases. Alphabetically arranged. Handwritten on printed forms. Condition poor. 292 pages. 14 x 8 x 1. County courthouse. Probate court storage, attic, south of elevator.

206. COST BILL
1887-1909. 3 volumes. (1-3) (Discontinued).
Itemized record of court costs in appointment of inventory appraisers. Alphabetically arranged. Handwritten on printed forms. Volumes average 320 pages. 14 x 8 x 1. County courthouse. Probate court storage, attic, south of elevator.

207. COST BILL
1896-1905. 2 volumes. (Discontinued).
Itemized record of court costs in sale of personal property. Alphabetically arranged. Handwritten on printed forms. Condition fair. Volumes average 250 pages. 14 x 8 x 1. County courthouse. Probate court storage, attic, south of elevator.

208. COST BILL
1898-1909. 3 volumes. (Discontinued).
Itemized record of court costs in probating wills. Alphabetically arranged.
Handwritten on printed forms. Condition fair. Volumes average 320 pages. 14 x 8
x 1. County courthouse. Probate court storage, attic, south of elevator.

209. COST BILL
1908-1909. 1 volume. (Discontinued).
Itemized record of court costs in lunacy inquest. Alphabetically arranged.
Handwritten on printed forms. 300 pages. 20 x 14 x 1. County courthouse. Probate
court storage, attic, south of elevator.

210. COURT COST, MISCELLANEOUS
1882-1908. 2 volumes. (2-3) (Discontinued).
Itemized record of court costs in miscellaneous cases; petitions, applications,
motions, and exceptions. Alphabetically arranged. Handwritten on printed forms.
Condition fair. 1 volume, 464 pages 20 x 10 x 2; 1 volume, 120 pages 20 x 10 x 1.
County courthouse. Probate court storage, attic, south of evaluator.

211. JURY BOOK
1883-1903. 1 volume.
List of jurors serving on probate court cases showing name, date, and fees.
Alphabetically indexed in back of volume. Handwritten on printed forms. Condition
poor. 320 pages. 12 x 10 x 1. County courthouse. Probate court storage, attic, south
of elevator.

212. WITNESS RECORD
1883-1917. 1 volume.
Record of witnesses appearing in court cases showing their names and amount of
fees. No index. Handwritten on printed forms. Conditioned poor. 404 pages. 12 x
8 x 2. County courthouse. Probate court storage, attic, south of elevator.

213. ACCRUED FEES
1909-1925. 7 volumes. (1-7).
Record of accrued fees showing in what matter, to whom charged, case number and amount. Alphabetically arranged. Handwritten on printed forms. Condition fair. Volumes average 238 pages. 20 x 12 x 1. County courthouse. Probate court office, west wall.

214. UNCLAIMED COST AND OTHER MONEYS PAID INTO COUNTY TREASURY
1885-1932. 1 volume.
Record of unclaimed moneys showing date and from what source received. Alphabetically arranged. Handwritten. Conditioned poor. 50 pages. 12 x 7 x .5. County courthouse. Probate court office, west wall.

215. UNCLAIMED DEPOSITS
1889-11892. 1 volume.
Reports filed in probate court by bank officials of unclaimed deposits of unknown depositors showing various amounts, dates, and names of depositors. Alphabetically arranged. Handwritten on printed forms. Condition fair. 348 pages. 20 x 14 x 2. County courthouse. Probate court storage, attic, south of elevator.

Maps

216. ATLAS AND DIRECTORY, TRUMBULL COUNTY
1899. 1 volume.
Printed atlas of Trumbull County showing various townships in colored maps; portraits and brief sketches of its early settlers and county officials; also list of freeholders and important centers of interest. Alphabetically indexed by names of topics. 236 pages. 18 x 16 x 1. County courthouse. Probate court office, west wall.

The county prosecutor, unlike the sheriff and coroner, is relatively one of the newer agencies in the administration of criminal justice. This office, established in America by the English during the colonial period, offers a striking difference in the development of American criminal procedures in contrast to the English where criminal prosecutions, in the main, were instituted by private persons. As developed in recent years, the office of prosecutor has become one of the state's most important agencies in its defense against modern crime.

The acts of the Northwest Territory placed the responsibility for criminal prosecutions upon the attorney-general, who, in turn, appointed and commissioned persons to prosecute cases in their respective counties.

While the act of the Northwest Territory outlined the local institutions for the newer states, the constitution of Ohio contained no provision for a prosecutor leaving its creation to the discretion of the legislature. In 1803, during the first session of the legislature, an act was passed authorizing the supreme court to appoint in each county of the state an attorney to prosecute cases in behalf of the state. (1 O. L. 50). Two years later the appointing power was vested in the court of common pleas. (3 O. L. 47). The office remained an appointive one until 1833 when the electors of the county were directed to elect a prosecutor in each county for a two-year term. (Chase, *op. cit.,* III, 1935; J. R. Swan, *Statutes of the State of Ohio,* Columbus, 1841, 737). The act of 1852 left the office elective and the term unchanged. In 1881 the term of office was set at three years, but it was reduced to two years in 1906. (78 O. L. 271-272).

Under the present system the prosecutor is elected for a four-year term. He is required to give bond of not less than one thousand dollars condition for the faithful performance of the duties of his office. In the event the office becomes vacant the court of common pleas is authorized to appoint a successor. In the case of disability the office is filled by an appointment by the county commissioners. (G. C. sec. 2,914-2,915).

The county prosecutor is authorized to appoint clerks, assistants, and stenographers and set their salaries. Since 1911, he has been authorized to appoint a secret service agent or officer whose duty it is to aid him in the collection of evidence to be used in a trial of criminal cases and in matters of a criminal nature. The compensation of such an officer is determined by the court of common pleas. (G. C. Sec. 2,914-2,915).

Most important among the duties of the prosecuting attorney are those connected with criminal prosecutions. These duties, differing little from the early days of the office, include the prosecution on behalf of the state of all complaints, suits, matters and controversies in which the state is a party, and such other suits, matters, and controversies as he is directed by law to prosecute within or without his county, in the probate court, court of common pleas, and court of appeals. In conjunction with the attorney general, he prosecutes cases in the supreme court which originate in his county. (G. C. sec. 2,916).

In felony cases, when a complaint is made to the prosecutor, he is required to examine the evidence and determine if it is sufficient for prosecution. If he decides in the affirmative, he prepares the evidence for presentation to the grand jury. If this body returns an indictment the prosecutor prepares to present the evidence in trial court. The court of common pleas may appoint an attorney to assist the prosecutor in criminal cases. (G. C. sec. 2,925). In the case of conviction, the prosecutor causes execution to be issued for the fines or cost and pays all moneys so received into the county treasury. (G. C. sec. 2,916).

Besides prosecution in criminal cases, the prosecutor also acts in civil matters. He may bring suit in the name of the state when he is convinced that public money is being misapplied or is being illegally withheld or withdrawn from the county treasury. Moreover, he may bring suit against persons violating the obligations of contracts of which the county is a party, or when county property is being used illegally or is illegally occupied. (G. C. sec. 2,921).

In addition to these, other duties have been prescribed by statute. On the request of the judge of the juvenile court, he must prosecute individuals for committing crimes against children. (G. C. sec. 1,664). Moreover, he must prosecute persons, when directed by the court of common pleas, for keeping a house of prostitution. (G. C. sec. 6,212, 6,215, 6, 217). At the investigation of the secretary of state, he must prosecute any officer who refuses to furnish gratuitously statistical information for the use of that office. (G. C. sec. 174).

The prosecutor has also served in an advisory capacity since 1881. (78 O. L. 260). He acts as an advisor to all county boards and officials and to township officers, who may require his opinion in writing on matters connected with their official duties. (G. C. sec. 2,917). In addition to this, he prepares official bonds for all county officers. (G. C. sec. 2,920).

The prosecuting attorney is required to make annually a report to the county commissioners stating the number of criminal prosecutions completed, the name or names of the party or parties to each, and the amount collected in fines, costs, and the amount forfeited. (G. C. sec. 2,925). Moreover on the demand of the attorney general he must make an annual report on all criminal actions prosecuted by indictment in his county, on forms provided by the state. (G. C. sec. 2,925; 78 O. L. 120; 90 O. L. 225).

217. CIVIL CASES
1925—. 12 file boxes.
Prosecutor's record of active and pending civil cases showing the name of each plaintiff, address, date filed, court action, disposition of case. Alphabetically arranged. Printed. 20 x 12 x 12. County courthouse. Prosecutor's office, west wall.

218. CRIMINAL CASES
1925—. 11 file boxes.
Prosecutor's record of active and pending criminal cases; also written evidence and dispositions showing the name of each defendant, address, and offense charged. Alphabetically arranged. 20 x 12 x 12. County courthouse. Prosecutor's office, west wall.

219. MISCELLANEOUS EVIDENCE
n. d. 48 foot shelving.
Pistols, knives, whiskey, and other articles obtained and introduced as evidence by the prosecuting attorney. No index. County courthouse. Prosecutor's office, north and south walls.

220. EVIDENCE
n. d. 2 file boxes.
Ropes, sledges, and other miscellaneous articles obtained and introduced as evidence by the prosecuting attorney. No index. 20 x 12 x 12. County courthouse. Prosecutor's office, north wall.

221. MISCELLANEOUS
n. d. 10 boxes.

Wood and cardboard boxes containing miscellaneous records belonging to the prosecutor's office. Nearly all boxes are tied and nailed and have insufficient markings. 24 x 20 x 12. County courthouse. Prosecutor's storage, attic.

222. OFFICERS' REPORTS
1850-1868, 1880-1882, 1910-1911. 3 volumes.

Annual reports of county officers pertaining to fines and costs in county prosecutions. No index. Handwritten on printed forms. Volumes average 175 pages. 14.66 x 8.66 x .66. County courthouse. Clerk's room, 4th floor.

The office of county sheriff, one of the oldest elective offices in America, had its inception in the Anglo-Saxon period of English history. (George Burton Adams, *Constitutional History of England,* New York, 1921, 17-19; W. A. Morris, "The Office of Sheriff in the Anglo-Saxon period," *English Historical Review,* XXXI, 19-40). As developed during the Anglo-Norman state, the sheriff, as the king's representative in the shire was empowered to collect taxes, conduct court, preserve order, and defend and protect the king's interest and prerogatives. But the arbitrary exercise of such extensive powers, together with the development of better methods of administration during thirteenth and throughout the centuries which followed resulted in a gradual reduction of his duties. At the beginning of the seventeenth century, although the sheriff continued to hold court in the shire for minor cases and presided at the sessions of the shire court for the election of members to parliament, he was in other respects little more than an executive agent of the courts bound to summon juries, execute judgments of the court, and administer the county jail. (Adams, *op. cit.,* 58, 87, 91. See also C. H. Haskins, *Norman Institutions, Harvard Historical Studies,* XXIV, 46).

The ancient institution, in modified form, was introduced in the American colonies; and as was natural, was continued by the states following independence. (For a comparative study of the sheriff in England and Chesapeake colonies, see Cyrus Harrold Kerraker, *The Seventeenth-Century Sheriff,* Chapel Hill, 1930). The office took on a new significance, when, in the latter part of the eighteenth century, a flood of colonists swept across the Alleghenies to establish homes in the Northwest Territory, as organized by congress in 1787. In the remoter west the pioneers, far removed from the orderly legal processes and courts of the east, were subjected to the machinations of a lawless element, as evidenced in every new community. In 1792 the governor and judges of the territory adopted an act which provided for the appointment, by the governor, of a sheriff in each county, and defined his duties. The sheriff was directed to keep and preserve the peace, suppress affrays, routs, riots, unlawful assemblies and insurrections; he was bound to apprehend, and confine in jail all felons and traitors; he was to return persons, who, after having committed a crime in his county, had taken refuge in another. In addition to this, he was directed to attend upon the court of common pleas and the court of appeals during their sessions, and, when directed, execute all warrants, writs, and processes to him directed by the proper lawful authority. (Pease, *op. cit.,* I, 8).

Ohio entered the union as a state in 1803. The office of sheriff was continued by constitutional provision, and was made elective for a two-year term. (*Ohio Const. 1802,* Art. V, sec. I). The constitution of 1851, although not specifically providing for the office, stated that no person shall be eligible to the office for more than four in any period of six years. (*Ohio Const, 1851,* Art. X, sec. 3). The term of office remained at two years until 1936 when it was extended to four years. (116 O. L. pt. 2, 1ˢᵗ secs. H. 603). The sheriff received his remuneration from fees, and not until 1906 was a definite salary specified by the legislature. (3 O. L. 49-51; 33 O. L. 18; 35 O. L. 53; 52 O. L. 86; 98 O. L. 95).

The duties of the sheriff were, and are, prescribed by statute. During the legislation of 1805 the general assembly passed an act defining the duties of the sheriff, which, in all respects, was similar to the provisions inherited from the territorial code. (3 O. L. 156-158). In the same year the sheriff was designated as the county's executor, and was bound to carry out sentences of death as imposed by the courts upon those convicted of murder. Hanging was the legal method adopted for the infliction of the death penalty. (Salmon P. Chase, *The Statutes of Ohio,* 3 volumes, Cincinnati, 1833-1935, I, 97-101; 109, 442-443). Public executions, the general rule during the earlier years, was abolished in 1844. (42 O. L. 71).

As in England the sheriff, during the earlier years of his office, was required to notify the electors of his county of the time and place of holding elections. He was required to furnish, at the expense of the county, ballot boxes; he was required to hold special elections when so directed by the governor; and was given the duty of delivering the poll books to the secretary of state. (2 O. L. 88-89; 3 O. L. 331-332).

An act of 1824, repealing the act of 1805, redefined the duties of the sheriff as a conservator of the peace in his county and as an executive agent of the courts. (29 O. L. 112). The present duties of the sheriff in this respect are survivals from the provision of this act. (29 O. L. 112-113; 82 O. L. 26). In the execution of his duties, as prescribed by law, he was empowered to summon to his aid such persons as he deemed necessary to perform his lawful duty. (29 O. L. 112-113). Thus the *posse comitatus* was at his disposal as it is today. Six years earlier, in 1818, the sheriff was authorized to appoint, with the consent of the court of common pleas, one or more deputies, who, like himself, were required to give bond for the faithful performance of the duties of their office. The sheriff was made responsible for their neglect of duty or misconduct in office. (29 O. L. 410).

Not only was the sheriff charged with the duty of apprehending law violators, but he was made responsible for their safekeeping. As early as 1803 he was made official custodian of the county jail. (3 O. L. 157). Although the early statutes directed the county commissioners to provide dungeons for the incarceration of prisoners, the act of 1847 directed the sheriff to exercise reasonable care for the preservation of the life, health, and welfare of those committed to his care. Indeed he was, and is, authorized to transport prisoners to other counties for safekeeping. (3 O. L. 157; 29 O. L. 112-113; 93 O. L. 131). In 1910 provision was made for the removal of the sheriff by the governor if he were proven guilty of negligence in affording a prisoner adequate protection from mob violence. (101 O. L. 109).

Although the sheriff is still regarded as the chief peace officer in the county, many of his earlier duties in this respect have been absorbed by the development of other agencies of law enforcement, notably the state highway patrol. On the other hand, the powers of the sheriff to suppress affrays, riots, and unlawful assemblies became especially important in the times of strikes or threatened riots. The sheriff, too, may arrest on a properly issued warrant any person charged with the ability of doing injury to another person or the property of another. (G. C. sec. 13,463). Moreover, since 1910 the sheriff has forwarded to the bureau of criminal identification all fingerprints of persons arrested for any felony (110 O. L. 5; 109 O. L. 585), And since 1913 has been authorized to arrest any prisoner violating his parole. (103 O. L. 405).

As an executive agent of the court the sheriff still executes all writs, warrants, and other processes directed to him by local authority; he attends the court of common pleas and court of appeals during their sessions, and, when required upon the probate court. (29 O. L. 112; 316; 82 O. L. 26; 103 O. L. 405).

Other historical functions of the sheriff have been altered or abolished. His duties regarding the announcement of elections long since have been taken over by the county board of elections. His duties regarding executions were absorbed by the state in 1886. (83 O. L. 145). Although the jury commission has supplanted the clerk of courts in the matter of selecting names of prospective jurors from the jury wheel, the sheriff's duties in this respect remain much as they were in the earlier years of his office.

The sheriff was, and is, required by law to keep a record of the business of his office. The present practice of keeping a foreign execution docket began in 1838. (36 O. L. 18; 57 O. L. 6; 84 O. L. 208-209).

Since 1843 the sheriff has kept a jail register (41 O. L. 74). And since 1868 a cash book. (65 O. L. 115; 84 O. L. 208; 86 O. L. 239). Indexes, direct and reverse to the foreign execution dockets, were prescribed by the legislature in 1925. (111 O. L. 31). Since 1843 the sheriff has been required, on the first Monday of September in each year, to submit to the county commissioners a certified statement of all fines and courts costs collected during the year in the amount of fees collected and paid to the clerk of courts of common pleas. (G. C. sec. 2,504; 41 O. L. 66; 48 O. L. 66). Moreover, since 1843 he has been required to transmit annually the jail register, in certified copies, to the clerk of courts, county auditor, and secretary of state. (41 O. L. 74).

The sheriff's records, public property and open to the inspection of the public, are transferred together with all effects appertaining to the office, to his successor.

Court Orders

223. FOREIGN DOCKET
1870—. 19 volumes. (1-19).

Foreign summons docket showing when writs were received and served giving case number, amounts of fees, mileage covered, names of attorneys, and amount of judgments. Alphabetically arranged. Handwritten on printed forms. Volumes average 324 pages. 18 x 14 x 1. County courthouse.

1870-1926, 11 volumes. Sheriff's file, 4th floor.

1927—, 8 volumes. Sheriff's office, west wall.

224. FOREIGN EXECUTION DOCKET
1910—. 3 volumes. (3-5).

Record of cases occurring outside Trumbull County showing the amount of judgment, names of plaintiff and defendant, amount of fees collected, and disposition of case. Alphabetically arranged. Handwritten on printed forms. Volumes average 452 pages. 14 x 12 x 3. County courthouse. Sheriff's office, west wall.

225. SERVICE RECORD
1924—. 8 volumes. (1-8).
Record of witnesses and jurors subpoened for court trials showing mileage covered, names of persons, and case number. Chronologically arranged. Handwritten on printed forms. Volumes average 358 pages. 16 x 12 x 1.5. County courthouse.
1924-1930, 4 volumes. Sheriff's file, 4th floor.
1931—, 4 volumes. Sheriff's office, west wall.

226. PARTITION RECORD
1877-1921. 2 volumes.
Record of real estate sales made by the sheriff and the settlement of estates showing the amount of each sale and cost in such actions. Alphabetically arranged. Handwritten. Volumes average 225 pages. 16 x 12 x 2. County courthouse. Sheriff's file, 4th floor, west wall.

227. SHERIFF'S SALES
1877-1880, 1897-1924. 4 volumes.
Record of real estate sold by the sheriff showing name of person to whom sold, amount of sale, and proof of publication. No index. Handwritten. Volumes average 400 pages. 12 x 10 x 1. County courthouse. Sheriff's file, 4th floor, west wall.

228. RECORD OF ARREST FOR TRAFFIC VIOLATIONS
1928. 1 volume. (Discontinued).
Record of arrest for traffic violations on county highways giving name of violators, address, place of violation, offense charged, time of arrest, and name of officer making arrest. No index. Handwritten. 250 pages. 18 x 12 x 2. County courthouse. Sheriff's office, west wall.

Records of Criminals, Crimes, and Accidents

229. CRIMINAL HISTORY
1935—. 2 volumes.
Record of known criminals giving name of each, aliases, last place of residence, and history. Alphabetically arranged. Typed on printed forms. Volumes average 250 pages. (loose-leaf) 18 x 15 x 2. County courthouse. Sheriff's office, west wall.

230. PHOTOGRAPHS AND FINGERPRINT FILE
n. d. 3 file boxes.

Criminal records furnished the sheriff by the Ohio and United States department of justice. Alphabetically arranged. 8 x 8 x 24. County courthouse. Sheriff's office, south wall.

231. JAIL REGISTRY
1894—. 7 volumes. (2-8).

Record of prisoners received at county jail giving name of each prisoner, name of arresting officer, charge, and time of arrival. Chronologically arranged. Handwritten on printed forms. Volumes average 200 pages. 18 x 12 x 1. County jail, High Street, sheriff's office, north wall.

232. ABANDONED CAR INDEX
1933—. 2 volumes,

Record of abandoned cars reported or found by the sheriff giving the make of each car, type, motor, and factory number, and place of abandonment. Alphabetically arranged. Typed on printed forms. Volumes average 200 pages. (loose-leaf) 12 x 8 x 1. County courthouse. Sheriff's office, west wall.

233. STOLEN CAR INDEX
1932—. 4 volumes.

Record of reports to the sheriff of stolen cars giving the date stolen, make and type of car, motor and factory number, and license number. Alphabetically arranged. Typed on printed forms. Volumes average 270 pages. (loose-leaf) 12 x 8 x 1. County courthouse. Sheriff's office, south wall.

234. ACCIDENTS
1935—. 1 volume,

Record of traffic accidents happening on county highways which were telephoned or otherwise reported to the sheriff's office showing the number of persons injured and killed giving the time and place of accident; also the weather condition. Alphabetically arranged. Typed on printed forms. 223 pages. 12 x 8 x 2. County courthouse. Sheriff's office, west wall.

235. MISCELLANEOUS
1931—. 8 file boxes.

Records of sheriff's sales, civil and criminal correspondence, notices of sales, deputies' bonds, and confiscated property. Arranged by names of topics. 12 x 12 x 21. County courthouse. Sheriff's office, west wall.

Cash Books, Fee Books, Journals, Etc.

236. SHERIFF'S CASH BOOK
1908-1918. 3 volumes. (1-3).

Record of cash received giving dates, amount, and amount turned over to county treasurer; also of money deposited in local banks, judgments, land sales, and court costs. No index. Handwritten. Volumes average 200 pages. 16 x 16 x 2. County courthouse. Sheriff's file, 4th floor, west wall.

237. CASH BOOK
1918—. 8 volumes. (1-8).

Record of all receipts and disbursements giving case number, from whom received, date, title of case, balance, amount paid, credits, to whom paid and date. No index. Handwritten. Volumes average 300 pages. 16 x 14 x 2. County courthouse. Sheriff's office, west wall.

238. DISBURSING CASH BOOK
1859-1887. 1 volume.

Records of all moneys paid out by the sheriff showing the dates, amounts, and to whom payable. Chronologically arranged. Handwritten. Condition poor. 180 pages. 12 x 10 x 1.5. County courthouse. Sheriff's file, 4th floor, west wall.

239. RECEIVING CASH BOOK
1859-1909. 2 volumes.

Record of fees collected showing costs in cases and names of plaintiffs and defendants. Chronologically arranged. Handwritten. Volumes average 360 pages. 14 x 10 x 1. County courthouse. Sheriff's file, 4th floor, west wall.

240. FEE BOOK
1894-1909. 4 volumes.

Record of all fees collected in the sheriff's office giving case number, names of plaintiff and defendant, date, and total cost. Alphabetically arranged. Handwritten on printed forms. Volumes average 446 pages. 16 x 12 x 2. County courthouse. Sheriff's file, 4th floor, west wall.

241. ACCRUED FEES
1907—. 8 volumes.

Record of fees collected by the sheriff in all cases giving case number, date, names of plaintiff and defendant, and cost. Chronologically arranged. Handwritten on printed forms. Volumes average 504 pages. 16 x 16 x 2. County courthouse.

    1907-1931, 5 volumes. Sheriff's file, 4th floor.

    1932—, 3 volumes. Sheriff's office, west wall.

242. BLOTTER
1894-1923. 9 volumes.

Sheriff's record of court cases showing names of plaintiff and defendant, docket number, and amount of fees. Chronologically arranged. Handwritten on printed forms. Volumes average 350 pages. 14 x 12 x 1. County courthouse. Sheriff's file, 4th floor, west wall.

243. CANCELED CHECKS
1925—. 7 file boxes.

Checks paid by the sheriff for various purposes showing the date, amount, to whom payable, and for what purpose. Chronologically arranged. 12 x 8 x 4. County courthouse. Sheriff's office, west wall.

244. BOUNTY FUND
1844-1886. 2 volumes.

Record of bounty funds paid to persons in Trumbull County for killing animals that were a nuisance and so prescribed by law giving name of person receiving bounty and the kind and number of scalps produced. It also contains the sheriff's accounts with Trumbull County, such as money collected in court cases, cost of trials, uncollected cost, and allowances made by the county commissioners in criminal cases. Chronologically arranged. Handwritten. Condition poor. Volumes average 200 pages. 12 x 8 x .5. County courthouse. Sheriff's file, 4th floor, west wall.

245. JOURNAL
1878-1909. 2 volumes.
Record of court cases giving list of jurors, amount of fees collected, and judgment rendered. Chronologically arranged. Handwritten. Volumes average 600 pages. 14 x 10 x 2. Condition poor. County courthouse. Sheriff's file, 4th floor, west wall.

246. UNCLAIMED MONEYS
1890-1906. 1 volume.
Record of moneys unclaimed and turned over to county treasurer; also certificates issued to owners and dates of claims. Alphabetically arranged. Handwritten on printed forms. 350 pages. 14 x 10 x 1. County courthouse. Sheriff's file, 4th floor, west wall.

While the acts of the Northwest Territory outlined the local institutions of the newer states, the first constitution of Ohio contained no provision for the office of county auditor, leaving its creation to the discretion of the legislature. It was not, however, until 1820 that the general assembly by joint resolution appointed a county auditor in each county for a one-year term. (18 O. L. 70). A year later the office became an elective one, and has so continued. (19 O. L. 116). The term of office was fixed at one year in 1821, two years in 1931, and three years in 1877. (19 O. L. 116; 29 O. L. 280; 74 O. L. 381). The term remained at three years until 1906 when it was reduced to two years. (98 O. L. 273). In 1919 the term of office was extended to four years. (108 O. L. pt. 2, 1294).

During the early years of his office the auditor was required, as he is today, to take an oath, give bond for the faithful performance of the duties of his office, and transfer to his successor all books, records, maps, and other papers appertaining to his office. (19 O. L. 116; R. S. 1033; G. C. sec. 2,559; 2,582). He was required, also, to preserve in his office all copies of entries, surveys, extracts, and other documents as may have been transmitted to his office from the auditor of state. (Chase, *op. cit.,* 1378). The auditor was authorized to appoint deputies to aid him in the performance of his duties. He and the sureties were, and are, liable for the official acts of his subordinates. Since 1869, a record of such appointments have been filed with the county treasurer. (G. C. Sec. 2,563; 66 O. L. 35). If the office were to become vacant the county commissioners were, and are, authorized to appoint some suitable person to fill the vacancy. (29 O. L. 280-291; 67 O. L. 103).

The first auditor in each county was required to list all lands subject to taxation lying within his county. From this list and a list submitted to him by the county commissioners and the state auditor, he was directed to make a tax duplicate to be kept in a book for that purpose. After completing the duplicate, he turned it over to the "tax collector," who in turn, proceeded, to demand payment. (18 O. L. 70). Moreover the auditor was directed to make a list from the treasurer's duplicate of all lands on which taxes were delinquent. In the event such lands were "sold for taxes" the auditor was authorized to grant a deed to the purchaser. (18 O. L. 70; 19 O. L. 116). Subsequent legislation expanded and itemized the duties of the auditor regarding taxation. During the decade of the forties the office of county assessors were abolished and provision was made for township assessors whose duty it was to list all taxable property in the township and make a return to the auditor. (39 O. L. 22-25).

Since 1874 the auditor has been required by statute, to keep a book in which he lists additions to and deductions from the amount of tax assessment. (71 O. L. 30). The auditor's duties regarding taxation have, with modifications to meet modern requirements, continued much as they were doing the earlier years of the office.

The county auditor, along with the county treasurer and county prosecutor, has served as a member of the county budget commission. As secretary to this body he is required to keep full and accurate records of the proceedings of the board. For the purpose of adjusting the tax rate and fixing the amount to be levied each year, the commissioners are governed by the amount of taxable property as shown on the auditor's tax list for the current year. The auditor submits to the commissioners the annual tax budget submitted to him by each taxing authority of each subdivision together with an estimate prepared by the auditor of state, of the amount of any tax levy, and other information as the budget commission may request or the state tax commission may require. (G. C. sec. 5,625-19; 112 O. L. 339).

Another important function of the county auditor has been the examination and approval of bills and other claims against the county before payment. Since 1831 the auditor has been authorized to issue all warrants on the county treasurer for moneys payable from the county treasury, upon the presentation of the proper voucher, and has been required to preserve all warrants showing the number, date of issue, amount for which drawn, in whose favor, and for what purpose and on what fund. (G. C. sec. 2,570; R. S. 1024; 29 O. L. 280-291; 67 O. L. 103). Money due to the state is paid on warrant of the auditor of state. (*Ibid.*, sec. 1,024). Since 1904 a bill or voucher for payment from any fund controlled by the county commissioners have been filed with the county auditor and entered in a book for that purpose at least five days before its approval for payment by the commissioners. When approved the date thereof is entered in such a book opposite the claim. (97 O. L. 25; 108 O. L. pt. 1, 266-272).

Besides approving bills and claims against the county, the auditor was early given the duty of certifying all moneys, except collections on tax duplicate, into the county treasury, specifying by whom paid and the funds to which such payment is credited. Such money he charges to the treasurer and keeps a duplicate in his office. Since 1835 all costs collected in penitentiary cases which have been paid by the state or which are to be so paid, have been certified to the treasury as belonging to the state. (33 O. L. 44; 67 O. L. 103).

The auditor, since 1831, has kept an account current with the county treasurer showing the payments of money into the treasury listing the time, by whom paid and from what fund. Upon receiving the treasurer's daily statement he was, and is, directed to enter on his account current as a charge to the treasurer the amount shown. (29 O. L. 280-291; 67 O. L. 103).

In 1902 the legislature made provision for a system of uniform accounting and auditing of all public offices, under the direction of a bureau of inspection in the auditor of state's office. The act provided, also, for the annual examination of the finances of all public offices. (95 O. L. 511-515). Since 1904 liquor taxes, cigarette taxes, and inheritance taxes have constituted separate funds. All other taxes are credited to the general fund. (97 O. L. 453). Semiannually the auditor makes a settlement with the treasurer asserting the amount of taxes the treasurer is to "stand charged." Semiannual settlements began in 1881; previous to that time settlements had been made annually. (G. C. sec. 2,596; 56 O. L. 128; 78 O. L. 226).

Since 1904 the auditor has been required to report to the commissioners on the state of county finances. On the first business day of each month the auditor prepares, in duplicate, a statement of the finances of the county for the proceeding month. After comparing it with the treasurer's balances, the statement is submitted to the commissioners, who, in turn, post one copy of it in the auditor's office where it remains for at least thirty days for the inspection and examination of the public. (67 O. L. 103; 97 O. L. 457).

During the development of the office other duties have been conferred upon the auditor with great diversity. For example, since 1833 he has been authorized to discharge from imprisonment, any person confined in jail for the nonpayment of any fine or amercement due to the county, when, in his opinion, the fine appears to be uncollectible. (G. C. sec. 2,576; 31 O. L. 18; 67 O. L. 103). The present day duty of reporting to the auditor of state statistics of death, dumb, blind, insane, and idiotic persons in his county with the names and post-office addresses of their parents or guardians, had its beginning in 1861. (58 O. L. 40). Eight years later saw the beginning of the practice of reporting to the same officer statistics of livestock in his county, as returned to his office by assessors, and an abstract of the funded and unfunded indebtedness of his county, and of each township, city, village, and school district. (G. C. sec. 2,604). During the same year, 1861, the auditor was given his present day duty of issuing peddlers' licenses to persons who filed a statement of his stock in trade in conformity with the law recording the listing of such stocks for taxation, and since 1917 he has issued dog licenses. (59 O. L. 67;

79 O. L. 96; 107 O. L. 34).

Besides his own duties, of which an incomplete account has been given, the auditor was early given the duty as serving as clerk to the county commissioners. He was, and is, required to keep an accurate record of their proceedings and preserve all documents, books, records, maps, and papers which might be required to be filed in his office. (G. C. sec. 2,566; 67 O. L. 103). Moreover, since 1850 he has been the official custodian of the reports submitted to the commissioners by the prosecuting attorney, the clerk of courts, the sheriff, and the treasurer. These reports have been recorded by the auditor in books kept especially for that purpose. (G. C. sec. 2,504; R. S. 886; 48 O. L. 66).

Then, too, since 1861 the auditor has served as the sealer of weights and measures, and is responsible for the preservation of the copies of the original standards delivered to his office. He enforces all state laws regulating weights and measures in his county. (G. C. Sec. 2,615; 85 O. L. 78; 101 O. L. 234).

In recent years there has been much criticism of the auditor's office. The chief complaint is, of course, that there is a duplication of work in the auditor's and in the treasurer's offices. The daily registers are, in all respects, similar.

Budget Commission

With the increased expenditures, following the World War, the need for improved methods of county finance administration became greater. This need was met, in 1927, by the establishment of a budget commission in each county. This commission, consisting of the county auditor, county treasurer, and prosecuting attorney, receives and examines the annual budget of the county, municipal, township and school authorities, with an estimate of the amount to be raised, for state purposes in each subdivision. (112 O. L. 399). If the total amount exceeds the amount authorized to be raised, the commission adjusts the amount to be raised, and may change and revise the estimates. The commission may reduce all items in the budget, but is prohibited from increasing the total of any budget or any item.

The adjusted budget is certified to the taxing authority in each subdivision. If the work of the commission is satisfactory, each taxing authority by ordinance or resolution authorizes the necessary tax levies and certifies them to the county auditor. (G. C. sec. 5,625-5,628).

On the other hand, the taxing authority in any subdivision may, through its fiscal officer, appeal from the decision of the budget commission to the state tax commission of Ohio which is empowered to adjust the estimates of revenues and balances in fixing the tax rate. (G. C. sec. 5,625-5,628).

Property Transfers

247. TRANSFERS
1812—. 35 volumes.
Record of transfers of titles to real estate showing names of persons concerned, description of property, date and location. Alphabetically arranged by names of townships; numerically arranged by range numbers. 1812-1861, handwritten; 1862—, typed on printed forms. Volumes average 300 pages. 20 x 14 x 3. County courthouse.
> 1812-1861, 5 volumes. Auditor's room, 4th floor.
> 1862—, 30 volumes. Auditor's office, south and west walls.

248. DEEDS
1855-1934. 1 volume.
Records of deeds given by the county auditor for the sale of real estate for taxes giving description and location of each property, date, to whom sold, and name of original owner. Alphabetically indexed. Handwritten. 250 pages. 16 x 12 x 1.5. County courthouse. Auditor's office, west wall.

Maps and Plats Books

249. MAPS
1928-1934. 35 maps.
Maps of county subdivisions, townships, and industrial districts. Prepared by county engineers for taxation purposes. No scale. 50 x 50. County courthouse. Auditor's office, south wall.

250. MAPS AND PLATS
1876. 1 volume.
Maps and plats of Trumbull County subdivisions and allotments showing exact location in acreage. Prepared by C. W. Tyler, county surveyor, for taxation

purposes. Scale, 1 inch equals one chain. 38 pages. 20 x 18. County courthouse. Auditor's office, west wall.

251. ATLAS AND DIRECTORY OF TRUMBULL COUNTY
1899—. 1 volume.
Printed publication containing maps, individual sketches, and brief biographies of leading Trumbull County citizens; also a list of freeholders, historical data, and a directory of Trumbull County officials from 1800 to 1898. Alphabetically arranged by names of topics. 235 pages. 24 x 20 x .5. County courthouse. Auditor's office, west wall.

Taxes

Appraisements and Assessments

252. ROAD ASSESSMENT RECORD
1802-1827, 1913-1933. 4 volumes.
Record of assessment for county roads and highways showing road number, estimated cost, contract price, location of road, names of owners who properties abut the road, and name of contractor making improvement. Alphabetically indexed. 1802-1827, handwritten; 1913-1933, typed. Volumes average 167 pages. 19 x 13 x 1.33. County courthouse. Auditor's office, west wall.

253. TAX DUPLICATE
1816—. 356 volumes.
Tax list of real property showing location, acreage, valuation, mileage, and total amount assessed. Chronologically and numerically arranged. 1816-1900, handwritten; 1901—, typed on printed forms. Volumes average 194 pages. 20 x 14 x 2. County courthouse.
    1816-1890, 67 volumes. Auditor's room, 4th floor, south wall.
    1891—, 289 volumes. Auditor's office, south wall.

254. APPRAISEMENT RECORD
1840-1935. 327 volumes.
Record of appraisements of real and personal property showing exact location and description, name and address of owner, and property valuation for taxation.

Alphabetically arranged by names of townships. Handwritten and typed on printed forms. Condition fair. Volumes average 180 pages. 18 x 12 x 1 and 118 pages 18 x 16 x 1.5. County courthouse.

    1840-1910, 145 volumes. Auditor's room, 4th floor.

    1911—, 182 volumes. Auditor's office, south wall.

255. RAILROAD LANDS
1853-1905. 1 volume.

Record of lands owned by railroads giving location, acreage, and total amount assessed. No index. Handwritten. Condition fair. 318 pages. 18 x 16 x 1.5. County courthouse. Auditor's office, west wall.

256. REVISION OF LOT NUMBERS
1870-1934. 18 volumes.

Auditor's record of revisions and changes showing lot number, names of owners, locations, acreages, and assessments. Alphabetically arranged by names of townships. Handwritten and typed. Volumes average 600 pages. 20 x 14 x 2.5. County courthouse.

    1870-1920, 11 volumes. Auditor's room, 4th floor, west wall.

    1921-1934, 7 volumes. Auditor's office, south wall.

257. ADDITIONS TO TAX DUPLICATE
1874-1931. 28 volumes.

Record of additional taxes assessed on real property showing date, name of property owner, amount assessed, and location. No index. Handwritten. Volumes average 250 pages. 20 x 20 x 1. County courthouse. Auditor's room, 4th floor, north wall.

258. DOG TAX DUPLICATE
1878. 1 volume.

Record of dogs taxed in Trumbull County giving name of owner, number of dogs, valuation, and amount assessed on each dog. Alphabetically arranged by names of townships. Handwritten. 320 pages. 20 x 14 x 2. County courthouse. Auditor's room, 4th floor, south wall.

259. LIQUOR ASSESSMENT DUPLICATE
1883-1915. 5 volumes. (1884-1912, missing).
Auditor's tax assessment on liquor dealers showing name and address of dealer, amount assessed, location, and taxable value of building where liquor was sold. Chronologically arranged. Handwritten on printed forms. Volumes average 206 pages. 18 x 12 x 1. County courthouse. Auditor's room, 4th floor.

260. ABSTRACT OF REAL PROPERTY
1890-1919. 28 volumes.
Abstract of real property valuation in Trumbull County showing lot number, exact location, and name of owner. Alphabetically arranged by names of townships. Handwritten on printed forms. Condition poor. 20 volumes average 200 pages 24 x 20 x 4; 8 volumes average 21 pages 24 x 18 x .25. County courthouse. Auditor's room, 4th floor, north wall.

261. LIQUOR DUPLICATE
1897-1903. 1 volume.
List of liquor dealers showing name and address of each property owner, location, property valuation, total assessment, and method of payments. Alphabetically arranged by names of townships. Handwritten on printed forms. 158 pages. 20 x 20 x 1.5. County courthouse. Auditor's room, 4th floor, south wall.

262. SANITARY DISTRICT ASSESSMENTS
1928-1935. 2 volumes.
Record of assessments against benefitted units in Mahoning Sanitary District showing amount of assessment against each unit. No index. Typed of printed forms. Volumes average 100 pages. (loose-leaf) 18 x 12 x 1. County courthouse. Auditor's office, south wall.

263. REAL ESTATE COMPLAINTS
1931—. 2 file boxes.
Record of complaints filed with county board of tax revision for readjustment of tax assessments listing date of each complaint and decision of the board. Numerically arranged by range numbers. Handwritten on printed forms. 24 x 15 x 12. County courthouse. Auditor's office, south wall.

264. INHERITANCE TAX CHARGE
1935—. 1 volume.

Record of inheritance taxes determined by probate court and charged against the estates giving name of estate and amount charged. Alphabetically arranged. Handwritten and typed on printed forms. 100 pages. (loose-leaf) 12 x 10 x 1. County courthouse. Auditor's office, west wall.

Delinquent Taxes

265. TAX SALE RECORD
1820-1840. 4 volumes. (A, 2-4).

Record and exact description of each property sold for delinquent taxes, showing location, valuation, and amount of tax due. Volume A also contains letters from state auditor governing sale of taxable properties. No index. Handwritten. Condition fair. Volumes average 200 pages. 18 x 12 x 2. County courthouse. Auditor's office, south wall.

266. DELINQUENT LAND TAXES
1840—. 32 volumes.

List of delinquent land taxes listing name of owner, location and valuation of property, tax rate, acreage, and total amount assessed. Alphabetically arranged by names of townships. 1840-1910, handwritten; 1911—, typed on printed forms. volumes (1840-1910) average 475 pages 20 x 20 x 2; (1911—.) 1100 pages 20 x 20 x 4. County courthouse.

> 1840-1926, 28 volumes. Auditor's room, south wall.
> 1927—, 4 volumes. Auditor's office, west wall.

267. DELINQUENT PERSONAL TAX
1876-1935. 11 volumes.

Auditor's list of unpaid taxes on personal property showing name of delinquent, list of properties, valuation, and total amount assessed. Alphabetically arranged by names of township. 1876-1904, handwritten on printed forms; 1905—, typed on printed forms. Condition fair. Volumes average 365 pages. 19 x 12 x 2. County courthouse.

> 1876-1929, 10 volumes. Auditor's room, 4th floor, south wall.
> 1930—, 1 volume. Auditor's office, west wall.

268. WHITTEMORE REMITS
1933-1934. 6 file boxes. (1-10932).
Treasurer's certificates of full payment of taxes after all the installments have been paid, as authorized by the Whittemore Act, each showing the date, certificate number, amount, and name of property owner. Numerically arranged. Handwritten on printed forms. 4 x 8 x 12. County courthouse. Auditor's office, north wall.

269. DELINQUENT SANITARY DISTRICT
1934-1935. 1 volume.
Record of assessments against benefitted units of the Mahoney Valley Sanitary District and certifications of the board of directors of unpaid levies. No index. Handwritten and typed on printed forms. 100 pages. 18 x 12 x 1. County courthouse. Auditor's office.

Tax Returns

270. SETTLEMENT PAPERS
1898-1917. 13 file boxes.
Records of additions to the tax duplicate, refunds, and statement of townships; also remits. Alphabetically arranged by names of townships. Handwritten on printed forms. 12 x 8 x 4. County courthouse. State examiner's office, west wall.

271. REMITTANCES
1902-1934. 3 file boxes.
Record of special assessments showing the date, amount, and source. Chronologically arranged. Typed on printed forms. 12 x 8 x 4. County courthouse. Auditor's office, west wall.

272. PERSONAL PROPERTY TAX RETURNS
1930—, 44 volumes.
Itemized list of all personal property showing name of owner, valuation, and amount assessed. Alphabetically arranged. Handwritten. Volumes average 620 pages, (loose-leaf), 16 x 10 x 3. County courthouse. Auditor's office, west wall.

273. NO TAX ESTATES
1932—. 8 file boxes.

Cost bill record of inheritance taxes as determined by the probate court. Chronologically arranged. Handwritten on printed forms. 12 x 8 x 4. County courthouse. Auditor's office, west wall.

274. COLLECTED INHERITANCE TAXES PAID
1935—. 1 file box.

Record of inheritance taxes as determined by probate court listing name of estate, amount taxed, date, and amount due. Numerically arranged. Typed on printed forms. 12 x 8 x 4. County courthouse. Auditor's office, west wall.

Elections

275. ELECTION STATEMENTS
1905—. 2 file boxes.

Statement of expenses incurred for holding elections in the various townships, showing date and total expense incurred for each. Alphabetically arranged by names of townships. Handwritten on printed forms. 4 x 8 x 12. County courthouse.

    1905-1934, 1 file box. State examiner's office.

    1935—, 1 file box. Auditor's office, west wall.

276. TOWNSHIPS AND OFFICERS ELECTED
1927-1933. 1 file box.

Statement of elected officials showing amount of fees and salaries collected. No index. Handwritten on printed forms. 4 x 8 x 12. County courthouse. Auditor's office, west wall.

Business and Administration of Office

Fiscal Accounts

277. JOURNAL
1805-1831. 1 volume.

Record of money collected and paid for road and other county improvements; also tavern licenses and stud horse fees. Chronologically arranged. Handwritten.

Condition fair. 225 pages. 15 x 10 x 1.5. County courthouse. Auditor's office.

278. SCHOOL SETTLEMENT RECORD
1831—. 4 volumes.

Record of county auditor's annual settlement with school district treasurers. The early volumes contain a record of settlements with townships which are now in Mahoning County. Alphabetically arranged by names of townships. Handwritten. Volumes average 274 pages. 15 x 10 x 1.5. County courthouse. Auditor's room, 4th floor, north wall.

279. APPORTIONMENT AND DISBURSEMENTS
1877—. 6 volumes. (1917-1932, missing).

Record of apportionment and disbursements of county funds to various townships, showing date, amount, from what source, and to which township. Chronologically arranged. Handwritten. Volumes average 150 pages. 20 x 18 x 1. County courthouse.

     1877-1916, 5 volumes. Auditor's room, 4th floor.
     1933—, 1 volume. Auditor's office.

280. TOWNSHIP AND CORPORATION RECORD
1904-1921. 3 volumes.

Auditor's record of accounts with various townships showing name of township, date, and amount of expenditure. Alphabetically arranged by names of townships. Handwritten on printed forms. Volumes average 598 pages. 20 x 12 x 2. County courthouse. Auditor's room, 4th floor, south wall.

281. DAILY BALANCE
1919-1931. 12 volumes.

Daily record of cash balance in county treasury as checked against approved expenditures by the auditor. Chronologically arranged. Handwritten on printed forms. Volumes average 318 pages. 10 x 8 x 1.5. County courthouse. Auditor's room, 4th floor, north wall.

282. FEES

1907—. 12 volumes. (1-12).

Daily record of all fees collected in auditor's office showing amount and source. Chronologically arranged. Handwritten on printed forms. Condition fair. Volumes average 310 pages. 18 x 12 x 2. County courthouse.

    1907-1928, 9 volumes. Auditor's room, 4th floor, north wall.

    1929—. 3 volumes. Auditor's office, west wall.

Bills

283. RECORD OF COMMISSIONERS' BILLS FILED

1904-1920. 3 volumes. (1-3).

Record of bills incurred by the board of county commissioners giving the date, amount, for what purpose, and to whom payable. Numerically arranged. Handwritten on printed forms. Condition fair. Volumes average 237 pages. 20 x 12 x 2. County courthouse. Auditor's room, 4th floor.

284. CLASSIFICATION OF BILLS PAID

1936. 1 volume.

Record of all funds spent for the operation of county offices showing amount and date of each expenditure. Alphabetically arranged. Handwritten on printed forms. 300 pages. 14 x 12 x 3. County courthouse. Auditor's office, west wall.

285. INDUSTRIAL COMPENSATION

1922—. 1 file box.

Record of expenditures for services of injured county employees authorized by workmen's compensation law and public work relief employees compensation law. Alphabetically arranged by names of townships. Typed on printed forms. 4 x 8 x 12. courthouse. Auditor's room, 4th floor, east wall.

286. INFIRMARY BILLS FILED

1904-1913. 1 volume.

Record of bills filed for the expenses of the county infirmary showing the date, to whom payable, and for what purpose. Numerically arranged. Handwritten on printed forms. 130 pages. 20 x 12 x 1. County courthouse. Auditor's room, 4th floor, north wall.

Fines

287. UNCLAIMED COST
1890—. 2 file boxes.
Reports of fines and costs collected by county clerk and justices of peace. No index. Handwritten on printed forms. 4 x 8 x 12. County courthouse. Auditor's office, west wall.

288. STATEMENT OF JUSTICES OF THE PEACE FINES
1920-1932. 1 file box.
Statement of fines collected by justices of peace. No index. Handwritten on printed forms. 4 x 8 x 12. County courthouse. Auditor's office, west wall.

Relief Records

289. SOLDIERS' RELIEF
1887-1897. 1 volume.
Record of minutes of meetings of soldiers' relief commission pertaining to the election of officials, amounts granted to indigent soldiers, sailors, and marines or to their wives, widows, or minor children. No index. Handwritten. Condition poor. 318 pages. 18 x 2 x 1.5. County courthouse. Auditor's room, 4th floor, north wall.

290 MOTHERS' PENSIONS AND BLIND RELIEF
2 file boxes.
Record of allowances made by probate court for the support of widows, minor children, and blind persons giving date and amount in each case. Chronologically arranged. Typed on printed of forms. 4 x 8 x 12. County courthouse.
　　1923-1932, 1 file box. State examiner's office, north wall.
　　1933—, 1 file box. Auditor's office, west wall.

291. MOTHERS' PENSIONS
1915-1931. 1 volume.
Record of moneys paid to mothers as authorized by probate court showing amount and to whom payable. Alphabetically arranged. Handwritten on printed forms. Condition fair. 170 pages. 18 x 14 x 2. County courthouse. Auditor's office, west wall.

292. BLIND RELIEF RECORD
1909—. 1 volume.

Record of warrants issued to blind persons showing number, amount, and to whom issued. Numerically arranged. Handwritten on printed forms. Conditioned poor. 300 pages. 10 x 8 x 1. County courthouse. Auditor's office, south wall.

293. EMERGENCY RELIEF
1933—. 2 volumes.

Record of orders issued for relief purposes showing name of person or firm to whom an order was issued, order number, date, amount, and for what commodity. Numerically arranged. Handwritten on printed forms. Volumes average 300 pages. 12 x 8 x 1. County courthouse. Auditor's office, south wall.

294. RELIEF
1933-1935. 167 file boxes. (170-42352).

Record of poor relief and relief orders showing name of recipient, amount, date, and for what commodity. Numerically arranged. Typed on printed forms. Condition fair. 12 x 12 x 24. County courthouse. Auditor's room, 4th floor, north wall.

295. RELIEF VOUCHERS
1933—. 20 file boxes. (1-18799).

Vouchers for relief bills showing date, amount, to whom payable, and for what purpose. Numerically arranged. Handwritten and typed on printed forms. 4 x 8 x 12. County courthouse. Auditor's office, west wall.

296. TRUMBULL COUNTY RELIEF COMMISSION
1933—. 4 volumes.

Auditors record of orders drawn on county treasurer for relief clients giving client's name, order number, date, to whom payable, amounts, and for what commodity. No index. Typed on printed forms. Volumes average 600 pages. 14 x 10 x 4. County courthouse. Auditor's office, north wall.

Vouchers and Warrants

297. VOUCHERS
1932—. 51 file boxes. (18850-62159).
Vouchers for payment of county bills showing number, to whom payable, amount, for what purpose, and from which fund. Numerically arranged. Handwritten and typed on printed forms. 5 x 10 x 24. County courthouse. State examiner's office, north wall.

298. ORDERS DRAWN ON COUNTY TREASURER
1801-1873. 7 volumes. (1823-1831, missing).
Records of orders drawn on treasury of Trumbull County showing date, to whom payable, amount, and for what purpose. Chronologically arranged. Handwritten. Condition poor. Volumes average 160 pages. 16 x 10 x 1. County courthouse. Auditor's office, west wall.

299. AUDITOR'S RECORD
1878-1904. 6 volumes.
Record of accounts showing warrants drawn, purpose, date, amount, and fund from which drawn. Numerically arranged. 1878-1889, handwritten; 1890-1904, typed on printed forms. Condition poor. Volumes average 532 pages. 20 x 24 x 2. County courthouse. Auditor's room, 4th floor, north wall.

300. COURT WARRANTS ISSUED
1904—. 3 volumes. (1918, missing).
 Record of warrants issued for common pleas and probate courts for witnesses, jurors, etc., each showing warrant number, amount, to whom payable, and for what purpose. Numerically arranged. Handwritten on printed forms. Condition fair. Volumes average 318 pages. 12 x 20 x 1. County courthouse.
  1904-1917, 1 volume. Auditor's room, 4th floor, south wall.
  1919—. 2 volumes. Auditor's office, west wall.

301. JOURNAL OF WARRANTS ISSUED
1911—. 18 volumes. (3-21).
List of warrants drawn on county treasury showing warrant number, amount, to whom payable, from what fund, and for what purpose. Numerically arranged.

Handwritten on printed forms. Volumes average 220 pages. 19 x 14 x 2. County courthouse.

  1911-1933, 15 volumes. Auditor's room, 4th floor, south wall.

  1934—, 3 volumes. Auditor's office, south wall.

302. JOURNAL OF WARRANTS ISSUED, JOURNAL OF PAYMENTS INTO COUNTY TREASURY
1874—. 8 volumes. (1877-1904, 1911-1917, missing).

Record of payments into county treasury showing date, amount, and from what source derived; warrants issued on county treasury showing date, amount, warrant number, to whom issued, purpose, and from what fund. Numerically arranged. Handwritten on printed forms. Condition fair. Volumes average 229 pages. 20 x 20 x 2. County courthouse.

  1874-1928, 6 volumes. Auditor's room, 4th floor, north wall.

  1929—, 2 volumes. Auditor's office, north wall.

Licenses and Permits

303. BEVERAGE LICENSES
1933-1935. 1 volume.

Record of licenses granted retailers to handle beverages showing name of dealer, date, location, and amount assessed. This record proceeded the sales tax. No index. Typed on printed forms (Ohio tax form 304A). 600 pages. 16 x 8 x 4. County courthouse. Auditor's room, 4th floor, north wall.

304. COSMETIC LICENSES
1933-1934. 1 volume.

Licenses granted wholesale and retail dealers handling cosmetics showing name of dealer, address, and date issued. This record proceeded sales tax. No index. Typed on printed forms (Ohio tax forms 3 and 4A). 300 pages. 16 x 8 x 2. County courthouse. Auditor's room, 4th floor, south wall.

305. DOG TAGS
1933—. 18 file boxes.

Applications and registrations of dog licenses showing name and address of applicant, description of dog, and amount assessed. Chronologically arranged.

Handwritten on printed forms. 4 x 8 x 12. County courthouse.
>1933-1935, 16 file boxes. State examiner's office, 4th floor.
>1935—, 2 file boxes. Auditor's office.

306. TRUMBULL COUNTY LIQUOR LICENSING BOARD
1916-1919. 1 volume.

Record of applications for liquor licenses authorized or rejected by the state board of liquor control showing the name and address of applicant, date of approval or rejection, and amount assessed; also license transfers, convictions for law violations, and appeals to state board. Alphabetically arranged. Handwritten on printed forms. 452 pages. 20 x 14 x 2. County courthouse. Auditor's room, 4th floor, north wall.

307. RETAIL CIGARETTE DEALER'S LICENSE
1927—. 9 volumes.

Retail dealers' licenses to traffic in cigarettes showing name of dealer, address, amount paid, license number, date of issuance, and date of expiration. Chronologically arranged. Typed on printed forms (Ohio tax form 3B). Volumes average 550 pages. 16 x 8 x 3.5. County courthouse.
>1927-1935, 7 volumes. Auditor's room, 4th floor, south wall.
>1935—, 2 volumes. Auditor's office, west wall.

308. VENDOR'S APPLICATIONS
1934—. 1 file box.

Record of vendors' applications for licenses to retail personal property giving name and address of vendor and date of application. Alphabetically arranged. Handwritten on printed forms (sales tax form number 1). 12 x 15 x 24. County courthouse. Auditor's office, south wall.

Financial Reports

309. LIBRARY ACCOUNT
1855-1861. 1 volume.

Complete record of libraries showing list of books purchased, dates, titles, purchase price each, and amount of money in each township fund. Alphabetically arranged by names of townships. Handwritten. 450 pages. 14 x 12 x 1.5. County courthouse. Auditor's room, 4th floor, north wall.

310. INSPECTORS' REPORTS
1876-1906. 1 volume.

Reports made by inspectors who have been authorized by probate judge to examine county treasury listing all deposits, drafts, bonds, and other moneys; also a record of recommendations made. Chronologically arranged. 1876-1900, handwritten on printed forms; 1900-1906, typed on printed forms. Condition fair. 240 pages. 18 x 14 x 2. County courthouse. Auditor's room, 4th floor, south wall.

311. FINANCIAL REPORTS
1910-1935. 2 file boxes.

Reports of the state auditor's department on financial conditions of Trumbull County treasury. No index. Typed on printed forms. 4 x 8 x 12. County courthouse. Auditor's office, west wall.

312. ANNUAL REPORT OF PROSECUTING ATTORNEY
1913-1929. 1 file box.

Annual statements of disbursements made by prosecuting attorney's office. Index. Typed on printed forms. 4 x 8 x 12. County courthouse. Auditor's office, west wall.

313. COUNTY DEPOSITORIES
1908—. 13 file boxes.

Record county funds deposited in local banks by county treasurer. No index. Handwritten on printed forms. 4 x 8 x 12. County courthouse. State examiner's office, west wall.

314. INTEREST
1903—. 27 file boxes.

Statement of interest accumulated on county funds in county depositories. Chronologically arranged. Handwritten on printed forms. 4 x 8 x 12. County courthouse.

> 1903-1930, 15 file boxes. State examiner's office.
> 1931—, 12 file boxes. Auditor's office, west wall.

315. DEBT SETTLEMENT
1923—. 12 file boxes.
Record of indebtedness of various school districts in Trumbull County. Chronologically arranged. Handwritten on printed forms. 4 x 8 x 12. County courthouse. Auditor's office, east wall.

316. SURPLUS FUNDS - CENTRAL ACCOUNTS
1841-1854. 1 volume.
Record of surplus revenue funds received from bond holders, each showing the amount, interest, and balance payable to county treasury. No index. Handwritten. Condition poor. 170 pages. 17 x 8 x 1. County courthouse. Auditor's office, south wall.

317. TAX RETURNS
1926—. 1 file box.
Record of annual tax returns of banks in Trumbull County. Chronologically arranged. Handwritten on printed forms. 4 x 8 x 12. County courthouse. Auditor's office, west wall.

Bonds

318. BONDS
1801-1877. 2 volumes.
Record of bonds given by county officials showing the name, date, amount, and date of expiration; also bonds of depositories for county funds and bonds of persons or firms handling explosives. Alphabetically arranged. Handwritten and typed. Condition poor. 422 pages. 20 x 12 x 2. County courthouse. Auditor's office, west wall.

319. BONDS
1896-1920. 2 volumes.
Record of bonds issued by county commissioners for the purpose of erecting the present courthouse and for the construction of bridges showing bond number, amount, and to whom sold. No index. Handwritten on printed forms. Volumes average 350 pages. 12 x 8 x 1. County courthouse. Auditor's room, 4th floor, north wall.

320. LIQUOR TRAFFIC RECORD
1882. 1 volume.
List giving names of liquor dealers, their addresses, and amount of bonds. No index. Handwritten on printed forms. 180 pages. 18 x 12 x 1. County courthouse. Auditor's room, 4th floor.

321. BOND RECORD
1904-1935. 4 volumes. (1-4).
Record of bonds issued and sold for improvement of county roads, bridges, and buildings, showing date, amount, and for what purpose; also total amount in each issue. Numerically arranged. Handwritten on printed forms. Condition fair. Volumes average 100 pages. 16 x 14 x 1. County courthouse. Auditor's office.

322. SCHOOL DISTRICT TREASURERS' BONDS
1923-1926. 1 file box.
Copies of bonds given by district school treasurers showing date, amount, and names of bondsmen. No index. Typed on printed forms. 4 x 8 x 12. County courthouse. Auditor's office, west wall.

323. SCHOOL CLERKS' BONDS
1931-1934. 1 file box.
Copies of bonds given by school clerks showing date, amount, and names of bondsmen. Chronologically arranged. Typed on printed forms. 4 x 8 x 12. County courthouse. Auditor's office, west wall.

324. TAX OFFICERS' BONDS
1915-1916. 1 volume.
Record of bonds and oaths of tax assessors of various taxing districts showing name of assessor, taxing district, and amount of bond. Alphabetically arranged. Typed on printed forms. 150 pages. 18 x 10 x 1. County courthouse. Auditor's office, west wall.

325. SURPLUS FUNDS ON INDIVIDUAL ACCOUNTS
1841-1850. 1 volume.
Record of bonds sold by states to individuals through county treasury showing amount, date, and name of purchaser; also a circular letter from state auditor to

county auditor and treasurer regarding collection of bonds. No index. Handwritten. Condition poor. 150 pages. 12 x 8 x 1. County courthouse. Auditor's room, 4th floor, north wall.

326. MISCELLANEOUS
1814-1935. 97 file boxes, 400 bundles and packages.
Miscellaneous bonds, agreements, school treasurer's settlements, expired bonds of county officials, deaf and dumb reports, Dow tax statements, blind relief reports, and other miscellaneous subjects. No index. Sizes vary from 4 x 8 x 25 to 12 x 16 x 48. County courthouse.

1814-1935, 400 bundles and packages. Auditor's room, 4th floor.

1814-1935, 97 file boxes. State examiner's office, north wall.

Budget Commission

327. BUDGET COMMISSION JOURNAL
1911—. 1 volume.
Minutes of meetings of budget commission and record of their valuation of real and personal properties. No index. Handwritten. Condition poor. 305 pages. 12 x 8 x 1. County courthouse. Auditor's office, south wall.

328. SCHOOL BUDGET
1929—. 11 file boxes.
Summary of amounts acquired from the general property tax approved by the budget commission and county auditor for county school operation. Chronologically arranged. Typed. 4 x 8 x 12. County courthouse. Auditor's office, west wall.

Miscellaneous

329. BRIDGE RECORD
1881-1888. 1 volume.
Record of bridges constructed in Trumbull County; also agreements with contractors for their construction showing the location, date, name of contractor, and estimated cost. Alphabetically arranged. Handwritten. Condition fair. 596 pages. 20 x 12 x 3. County courthouse. Auditor's office, south wall.

330. ANIMAL CLAIMS
1918-1935. 1 volume.

Record of animal claims filed with the county auditor showing name of claimant, number of animals killed or an injured, names of witnesses, and dates. No index. Handwritten on printed forms. 75 pages. 18 x 10 x .5. County courthouse. Auditor's office, west wall.

331. SEALERS' RECORD
1912-1921. 2 volumes.

Record of scales and measures inspected by the county sealer showing date and name of person or firm. Arranged by months. Handwritten on printed forms. Volumes average 101 pages. 14 x 14 x 1. County courthouse. Auditor's room, 4th floor, north wall.

The office of county treasurer, established by an act of the Northwest Territory in 1792, was continued by the state of Ohio. (Pease, *op. cit.,* 68-69). Although the constitution of 1802 made no provision for the office of county treasurer, it was created by the legislative act of 1803. (1 O. L. 98). The treasurer, appointed by the associate judges in 1803 and by the county commissioners in 1804, was required to take an oath; give bond for the faithful performance of the duties of his office; and was subject to removal by the appointing power. (1 O. L. 98; 2 O. L. 154). The treasurer remained an appointive official until 1827, and after that date an elective one by popular vote in the county. (25 O. L. 25-32). The constitution of 1851, although not specifically creating the office, stated that no person shall hold the office of treasurer for more than four years in any six. (*Ohio Const. 1851,* Art. X, sec. 3. This provision was repealed in 1933, with the adoption of an amendment authorizing any county to adopt a charter form of government). The legislature, interpreting the constitutional provision, fixed the term of office at two years in 1859. (59 O. L. 101). The term of office continued at two years until 1935 when it was extended to four years. (116 O. L. pt. 2, 1st s. sess. H. 603). Until 1906 the county treasurer received his remuneration from fees, since that date his salary has been determined by law, according to the population of the county.

Although the duties of the treasurer were defined by statute in the earlier period, the act of 1827 and act of 1831, repealing the previous acts, defined his duties in detail. The provisions of the latter act, although subject to amendment and repeal, furnished the basis for subsequent legislation and laid the basis for the present-day duties of the treasurer, which, in the main, do not differ greatly from those prescribed by the earlier statutes.

In 1803 the treasurer was given the present day duty of giving public notice of the tax duplicate. Upon receiving from the county auditor a duplicate of the taxes assessed upon the property of the county, the treasurer prepares notice to be posted in three places in each township, one, the place in which elections are held. Also, the notice is inserted for six consecutive weeks in the newspaper having the greatest circulation in the county. (1 O. L. 98; 29 O. L. 291; 52 O. L. 124). He receives money and payment of taxes levied for the county, state, and for other purposes; giving the person so paying, a receipt. (G. C. sec. 2,650; 29 O. L. 291; 76 O. L. 70; 85 O. L. 327). In the earlier years of the office the treasurer was required to give announcement for the time he would be in the respective townships of the county and in his office at the seat of justice to receive tax collections. Since 1858 the treasurer has been authorized to prescribe the semiannual payment of taxes or assessments levied upon real estate or upon delinquent real estate taxes or assignments. (55 O. L. 62; 56 O. L. 101). Moreover, since 1908 the commissioners have been authorized to extend the time of paying taxes for not more than thirty days after the time fixed by law. (99 O. L. 435; 114 O. L. 730; 115 O. L. pt. 2, 226).

The treasurer is required to report to the auditor after each semiannual collection of taxes, showing the amount of taxes received at each taxing district in the county since the last settlement. Since 1904 the semiannual settlements have been made under the heads of liquor taxes, cigarette taxes, inheritance taxes, delinquent personal taxes, road taxes, and general taxes. The treasurer keeps his accounts in books enabling him to compile such reports. (G. C. sec. 2,643; 29 O. L. 296; 97 O. L. 458).

After the taxes are collected and immediately after each settlement with the county auditor, the county treasurer, upon the presentation of the proper warrant from the auditor, pays to the township treasurer, city or village treasurer, the treasurer of the school district, or treasurer of any legally constituted board authorized by law to receive the funds or proceeds of any special tax levy, or other officer delegated with the authority to receive such funds, all moneys in the county belonging to such boards and subdivisions. (G. C. sec. 2,689; R. S. 1122; 56 O. L. 101). Then, too, after the treasurer has made each settlement with the county auditor, he is required to pay to the state treasurer, on warrant from the state auditor, the full amounts of all sums found by the state auditor to belong to the state. (56 O. L. 101; 114 O. L. 732).

The treasurer is required to keep an account current with the county auditor. This practice originated in 1831. Each day the treasurer makes a statement to the county auditor for the previous day's business showing the amount of taxes received on auditor's drafts, the amount received from other sources, together with the amount of money deposited in the depository, the total amount paid out by check and by cash, and the balance in the treasury. (G. C. sec. 2,642; 55 O. L. 44; 97 O. L. 458).

Another function of the county treasurer, having its inception in the earlier years of the office, is the collection of delinquent taxes. It was, and is, his duty to assess a penalty on the tax duplicate for the non-payment of taxes, which penalty when collected is paid into the treasurer's fund. If the treasurer is unable to collect the delinquent taxes, he is authorized to apply to the clerk of courts of common pleas, and the clerk serves notice to show cause why such taxes were not paid. The court may enter a rule against the delinquent taxpayer for the payment and cost and enforce it by attachment. (56 O. L. 175; 99 O. L. 435).

During the last decade provision has been made whereby delinquent taxes, assessments and penalties charged on the tax duplicate against any entry of real estate may be paid in installments during the five consecutive semiannual taxpaying periods, whether such real estate has been certified as delinquent or not. (G. C. sec. 2,672; 114 O. L. 827). The Whittemore act, passed in 1936, provides for the collection of the delinquent real estate taxes and assessments, personal property and classified property taxes prior to 1935, by installments. (S. B. 359 1st s. sess. 1935, *Baldwin's Ohio Code Services,* Oct., 1936, 10). In some of the more populous counties the treasurers maintain a separate bureau for the collection of delinquent taxes.

The county treasurer has charge of the funds collected by taxes, and also of other funds belonging to the county. Although earlier acts made provision for storage vaults in the county treasury for county deposits, the commissioners have been authorized, since 1894, to receive sealed bids for the deposit of county funds and the bank or trust companies offering the highest rate of interest are selected as the county depositories. (91 O. L. 403; 102 O. L. 60; 115 O. L. pt. 2, 215).

The treasurer, as well as the sheriff, the prosecutor, and the clerk, is required to report annually to the county commissioners. Since 1874 the county auditor and county commissioners have been required to make a thorough examination of all books, vouchers, accounts, moneys, bonds, securities and other property in the treasury at least every six months. (G. C. sec. 2, 699; R. S. 1129; 71 O. L. 137). The treasurer, besides being under the supervision of the county commissioners and county auditor, is subject to the supervision of the state auditor. In 1902 an act was passed providing for a uniform system of accounting and auditing for all public offices in the state, under the direction of a bureau of inspection in the office of the state auditor. The act provides, also, for the annual examination of the finances of all public offices. (G. C. sec. 2,641; 114 O. L. 728; R. S. 1084).

The treasurer, like other county officials, is required to turn over to his successor all books, papers, moneys, and records appertaining to his office. Since the inception of the office the treasurer has been the official custodian of the bonds furnished to the state by the county auditor, county commissioners, county sheriff, etc.

The treasurer, like other county officials, is required to turn over to his successor all books, papers, moneys, and records pertaining to his office. Since the inception of the office the treasurer has been official custodian of the bonds furnished to the state by the auditor, commissioners, sheriff, etc. Since 1869 he has been required to record and preserve a record of the deputies appointed and removed by the county auditor. (G. C. sec. 2,563; 66 O. L. 35).

The treasurer is a member of the budget commission and county board of review. (G. C. sec. 5,625-19; G. C. sec. 5,580).

Tax Records

Assessments and Receipts

332. TAX DUPLICATE
1804-1936. 585 volumes.

Duplicates of real property taxes giving name of each owner, location, acreage, tax rate, and amount due. Alphabetically arranged by names of townships; also numerically arranged by range numbers. 1804-1900, handwritten; 1901-1936, typed on printed forms. Many of the early volumes are in poor condition. Volumes average 100 pages. 12 x 6 x .5 to 300 pages 20 x 20 x 3. County courthouse.

1804-1927, 501 volumes. Treasurer's storage, attic.
1928-1929, 20 volumes. Surveyor's room, 4th floor.
1930-1936, 64 volumes. Treasurer's office.

333. SCHOOL FUNDS AND ENUMERATION
1851-1913. 4 volumes.

List of white and colored pupils (male and female) in various township schools and a record of the amount of taxes assessed for school purposes. Chronologically arranged. Handwritten. Volumes average 528 pages. 16 x 8 x 1. County courthouse. Treasurer's storage, attic.

334. LIQUOR DUPLICATE
1883-1884. 1 volume.

Records name and address of each person engaged in the sale of intoxicating liquors, amount of assessment, and distribution of tax collected. Alphabetically arranged. Handwritten. 188 pages. 20 x 14 x 1. County courthouse. Treasurer's storage, attic.

335. LIQUOR DUPLICATE
1884-1914. 8 volumes.

Treasurer's duplicate of assessments on the sale of intoxicating liquors giving the name of each person so engaged, name of property owner, location and description of premises where liquor was sold, and amount of assessment. Alphabetically arranged by names of township. Handwritten on printed forms. Volumes average 100 pages. 20 x 18 x 1.5. County courthouse. Treasurer's storage, attic.

336. SPECIAL TAX DUPLICATE
1891-1936. 65 volumes.

Record of special taxes levied for county improvements giving location, description, and valuation of each property assessed. Arranged by townships and ranges. 1891-1922, handwritten; 1923—, typed on printed forms. Volumes average 300 pages. 20 x 18 x 2. County courthouse.

    1891-1929, 49 volumes. Treasurer's storage, attic.

    1930-1936, 16 volumes. Treasurer's office, south wall.

337. CIGARETTE DUPLICATE
1909—. 5 volumes.

Records of assessments on cigarette business giving amount assessed, name and address of dealer, certificate number, and date of expiration. Alphabetically indexed by names of townships. Handwritten on printed forms. Volumes average 200 pages. 18 x 11 x .5. County courthouse.

    1909-1924, 3 volumes. Treasurer's storage, attic.

    1925—, 2 volumes. Auditor's office.

338. LIQUOR TRAFFIC ASSESSMENT DUPLICATE
1921-1931. 1 volume. (Discontinued).

Record of fines and assessments on real estate for liquor law violations giving each tenant's name, property owner's name, location, and general description of premises where intoxicating liquor was sold. No index. Handwritten on printed forms. 100 pages. 16 x 12 x 1. County courthouse. Treasurer's office, north wall.

339. CLASSIFIED TAX DUPLICATE
1932-1936. 4 volumes.

List of productive investments, accounts taxable, and amount assessed. No index. Typed on printed forms. Volumes average 154 pages. 20 x 18 x 1. County courthouse. Treasurer's office, east wall.

340. INHERITANCE TAX CHARGES
1932—. 1 volume.

Record showing amount of inheritance tax on taxable estates determined by probate court and charged to county auditor. Alphabetically arranged. Typed of printed forms. Condition fair. 200 pages. 12 x 12 x 2. County courthouse. Treasurer's office, south wall.

341. DUPLICATE TAX STATEMENTS
1935—. 1,228 file boxes.

Tax statements for the last half of 1935 showing property owner's name, rate of tax, and amount due semiannually. Alphabetically indexed by names of townships. Handwritten on printed forms. 3 x 6 x 8. County courthouse. Treasurer's office, center of room.

342. INVENTORY AND SALES TAX RECEIPTS
1935—. 1 volume.

Daily record of sales tax stamps sold showing denomination, amount on hand, and amount received from state. No index. Handwritten on printed forms. 100 pages. 20 x 16 x 1. County courthouse. Treasurer's office, south wall.

343. DUPLICATE TAX STUBS
n. d. 50 boxes.

These wooden and cardboard boxes contain many thousand stubs of tax statements showing each taxpayer's name, rate, and amount of taxes paid. The stubs are in boxes, not filed in any particular manner, generally thrown in. Condition poor. Sizes of boxes vary from 20 x 16 x 8 to 36 x 24 x 24. County courthouse. Treasurer's storage, attic.

Delinquent Taxes

344. TAX SALE RECORD
1840-1871. 1 volume.
List of taxable properties sold to county treasury for delinquent taxes giving description of each, location, acreage, and amount due. No index. Handwritten. Condition fair. 400 pages. 14 x 10 x 1. County courthouse. Treasurer's storage, attic.

345. DELINQUENT SANITARY ASSESSMENT BOOK MAHONING VALLEY SANITARY DISTRICT
1928—. 2 volumes.
Record of assessments and delinquent taxes on real estate in Mahoning Valley Sanitary District only. No index. Typed on printed forms. 20 x 18 x 1. County courthouse. Treasurer's office, north wall.

346. COUNTY TREASURER'S CUMULATIVE DELINQUENT DUPLICATE TAXES OTHER THAN REAL ESTATE
1932-1936. 9 volumes.
Record of accounts of personal properties showing amount of taxes and penalties assessed, name and address of each person, location, and year entered. Alphabetically arranged. Typed. Volumes average 800 pages. 12 x 10 x 5. County courthouse. Treasurer's office, east wall.

347. WHITTEMORE
1934-1936. 2 volumes.
Treasurer's record of undertakings to pay taxes on installment plan showing name of each person, description of property, amount due, and payment plan. Numerically arranged. Handwritten on printed forms. Volumes average 350 pages. 20 x 10 x 2. County courthouse. Treasurer's office, east wall.

Business and Administration of Office

Cash Books, Journals, and Ledgers

348. CASH BOOK
1893—. 9 volumes.
Records of all receipts and disbursements; also weekly cash balance in county treasury. No index. Handwritten on printed forms. Condition fair. Volumes average 164 pages. 20 x 14 x 1. County courthouse.

1893-1904, 4 volumes. Treasure's storage, vault.

1905—, 5 volumes. Treasurer's office.

349. DAY BOOK
1835-1856. 3 volumes.
Daily record showing amount of money collected by county treasury. No index. Handwritten. Condition poor. Volumes average 100 pages. 14 x 6 x .5. County courthouse. Treasurer's storage, attic.

350. TREASURER'S RECORD OF FEES
1907-1925. 3 volumes.
Record of taxes refunded giving name of owner, date of payment, and amount refunded. See entry 348 for record of fees after 1925. Alphabetically arranged. Handwritten. Condition fair. Volumes average 152 pages. 12 x 6 x 1. County courthouse. Treasurer's storage, attic.

351. JOURNAL RECEIPTS INTO TREASURY
1917—. 5 volumes.
Record of all receipts of county treasury showing date, amount, from what source, and to which fund credited. Numerically arranged. Handwritten on printed forms. Volumes average 100 pages. 20 x 16 x 1. County courthouse.

1917-1927, 3 volumes. Surveyor's room, 4th floor.

1928—, 2 volumes. Treasurer's office, west wall.

352. JOURNAL
1933—. 3 volumes.
Record of expenditures for poor relief listing each warrant number, date issued, amount, and to whom issued. Numerically arranged. Handwritten on printed forms. Volumes average 300 pages. 14 x 10 x 1. County courthouse. Treasurer's office, west wall.

353. TREASURER'S RECORD
1878—. 8 volumes.
Record of orders redeemed by county treasury showing amount of order, date, and to whom issued. Numerically arranged. Handwritten. Condition poor. Volumes average 271 pages. 24 x 20 x 2. County courthouse.
    1878-1917, 6 volumes. Treasurer's storage, attic.
    1918—, 2 volumes. Treasurer's office, west wall.

354. JOURNAL OF WARRANTS REDEEMED
1832—. 24 volumes.
Record of warrants redeemed by county treasurer showing date, to whom issued, amount, for what purpose, and from which fund. No index. Handwritten. Volumes average 250 pages. 20 x 14 x 2. County courthouse.
    1832-1931, 19 volumes. Treasurer's storage, attic.
    1932—, 5 volumes. Treasurer's office, west wall.

355. LEDGER
1904—. 5 volumes.
Record of all funds received by county treasurer from various county departments giving date, amount, and from what source. Alphabetically arranged. Handwritten on printed forms. Volumes average 300 pages. 16 x 14 x 2. County courthouse.
    1904-1912, 1 volume. Treasurer's storage, attic.
    1913—, 4 volumes. Treasurer's office, west wall.

Miscellaneous

356. SCHOOL FUND SETTLEMENT WITH SCHOOL TREASURERS
1838-1911. 6 volumes.
Township school treasurers' settlements with county treasurers showing name of

teachers, amount of salaries, and other school expenditures. Alphabetically arranged by names of townships. Handwritten. Condition fair. Volumes average 540 pages. 18 x 8 x 2. County courthouse. Treasurer's storage, attic.

357. INSPECTOR'S REPORTS OF TREASURER'S OFFICE
1876-1930. 5 volumes. (1916-1926, missing).

State examiner's reports of county offices showing financial condition and recommendations made. No index. Handwritten. Condition poor. Volumes average 122 pages. 16 x 10 x .5. County courthouse. Treasurer's office, west wall.

358. BONDS
1890—. 2 volumes.

Record of bonds of elected county officials showing amount, signatures of witnesses, and approval of county commissioners. Alphabetically arranged. Handwritten on printed forms. Condition poor. Volumes average 200 pages. 18 x 10 x 1. County courthouse. Treasurer's office, west wall.

359. TOWNSHIP CLERKS' BONDS
1923-1935. 1 volume.

Record of township clerks bonds showing amount, name of bonding company, and approval by township trustees. Alphabetically arranged. Handwritten on printed forms. 102 pages. 16 x 8 x .5. County courthouse. Treasurer's office, west wall.

The office of county surveyor (now the county engineer), another English institution transplanted in America during the colonial period, became an important office in colonial Ohio where land titles and boundary lines were often in dispute. The office is purely a creature of statute there being no constitutional provision for its establishment.

The first act of the general assembly pertaining to the surveyor was passed during the first legislative session of 1803. Under this act the court of common pleas was authorized to appoint a person well qualified to act as county surveyor. He received his commission from the governor, was required to give bond conditioned for the faithful performance of the duties of his office; and was directed to survey all lands which were sold or were to be sold for taxes. The surveyor was authorized to appoint chainmen or markers whose function it was to establish corners. The surveys made by the surveyor or his deputies were the only ones to be accepted as legal evidence in any court of law or equity. For remuneration, the surveyor was permitted to retain all fees collected by him in the operation of his office. (1 O. L. 90-93).

The act of 1816, although making no fundamental change in the duties of the surveyor, fixed his term of office at five years; authorized him to appoint deputies and made him responsible for their official acts. Moreover, he was made liable to removal by the court for negligence or incompetency, and was made liable to a suit by persons believing themselves damaged by his negligence or the negligence of his deputies. (14 O. L. 224-225). A year later, in 1817, provision was made for the appointment of a successor in the event the office became vacant due to death, resignation, or removal. (15 O. L. 65).

The act of 1831 consolidated the previous acts, redefined the duties of the surveyor, increased the amount of his bond, and authorized him, when directed by the county commissioners, to procure from surveyor general's office a certified plat together with the field notes. It provided further, that the surveyor should keep "a fair and accurate record of all official surveys made by himself or by his deputies," in a suitable book to be kept by him for that purpose; and that he should number his surveys progressively. (29 O. L. 402). More significant however was the fact that the office was made elective for a three-year term by the act of 1831. The term remained at three years until 1906 when it was to be reduced to a two-year period. (29 O. L. 399; 98 O. L. 245-247).

During the years of the development of the office other duties have been delegated to the surveyor. Thus in 1842 he was given the duty of ascertaining and reporting trespassing on public lands. (40 O. L. 57). Two years later he was given the same powers as the justices of the peace to take and certify deeds, mortgages, powers of attorney, and other instruments affecting real estate, to administer oaths, and take affidavits and to certify them. (52 O. L. 70). In 1867 he was given authority, when directed by the county commissioners, to transcribe any and all dilapidated maps, records of plats, and field notes of surveys and other counties. (64 O. L. 216-217; 78 O. L. 258). Similarly, in 1881, he was authorized to procure from any office in the state a certified plat together with the field notes of corners, quarter sections, lot or original survey and placed them in a book provided for that purpose. Certified copies from his book to be taken as *prima facie* evidence. (29 O. L. 399; 78 O. L. 285).

With the increase in modern means of transportation there was a growing need for more efficient methods of road construction and maintenance. Accordingly, in 1906, the surveyor was directed to act, whenever the service of an engineer was required, in the capacity of an engineer with respect to roads, turnpikes, bridges, or ditches, except in cities of the first grade. (98 O. L. 245-247). Fourteen years later he was directed by statute to perform all duties in his county which would be done by a civil engineer or surveyor. He was directed further to prepare all plans, specifications and estimates of cost, and submit forms of contracts, for the construction and repair of all bridges, culverts, roads, draws, ditches, and other public improvements (except buildings) over which the county commissioners had authority. He was, at the same time, made responsible for the inspection of all public improvements, and was directed to keep a complete list of all estimates and bids received for such work as well as contracts awarded for improvement. (98 O. L. 245-247).

Similarly another measure, enacted in 1919, increased the duties of the surveyor regarding road construction and road maintenance. Under this act the surveyor was authorized to designate one of his deputies as maintenance engineer. This engineer, under the direction of the surveyor, was to have charge of all "road maintenance and road work" in his county. It was provided further that the surveyor, when authorized by the county commissioners, was to appoint a maintenance supervisor or supervisors to have charge of the maintenance of improved highways within a district or districts established by the commissioners or surveyor, and contain not less than ten miles of improved county roads. (108 O. 1. pt. 1, 497).

Four years later the surveyor was given the additional duty of assisting the county planning commission. (110 O. L. 312),

Thus the general responsibility of planning and directing county road construction is vested, by statute, in the county surveyor. With this increased responsibility placed on this office there has been an attempt made to raise the general qualifications of those seeking election to it. Accordingly, in 1935, an act was passed changing the title of the office to that of "county engineer," and eligibility to the office was restricted to "professional and registered surveyors listed to practice in the state of Ohio." (116 O. L. 283). This act was amended in 1936 to permit the incumbent to continue in office upon re-election, despite the lack of these qualifications.

Bridge, Ditch, Road, and Sewer Records

360. DITCH RECORD
1861-1923. 5 volumes. (1-5).
Record of petitions to county commissioners for ditches and improvements giving engineer's estimate of cost, location, length, and notices to contractors of improvements to be made. Alphabetically arranged. Handwritten. Volumes average 403 pages. 14 x 10 x 1.5. County courthouse. Surveyor's office, west to wall.

361. ESTIMATES
1912-1930. 3 volumes.
Estimates of labor and material required for repair of roads, bridges, and ditches giving location of project, description, and amount of contractor's bids. Alphabetically arranged. Handwritten. Volumes average 198 pages. 16 x 12 x 1. County courthouse.
    1912-1913, 1 volume. Surveyor's storage, attic.
    1917-1930 2 volumes. Surveyor's office, west to wall.

362. ROAD RECORD
1802-1934. 7 volumes. (1-7).
Record of petitions to county commissioners for construction of roads and road improvements giving location and length of each road; also notices to owners whose properties abut road to be improved. Record also contains resolutions for views and hearings, proofs of publication of notices, and engineers estimate cost of such

improvements. Alphabetically arranged. Handwritten. Volumes average 398 pages. 16 x 12 x 2. County courthouse. Surveyor's office, west to wall.

363. MAINTENANCE AND REPAIRS
1828-1919. 3 volumes. (1863-1911, missing).
Record of road repairs giving location, description, and kind of material used; also cost of material and labor. Alphabetically arranged. Handwritten. Volumes average 196 pages. 16 x 12 x 1. County courthouse.
> 1828-1862, 1 volume. Surveyor's office, west to wall.
> 1911-1919, 2 volumes. Surveyor's storage, attic.

364. CONSTRUCTION RECORD
1916-1931. 1 volume.
Record of roads constructed and repaired showing name, location, length, description, number, and kind of materials used. Alphabetically arranged. Handwritten. 225 pages. 16 x 13 x 2. County courthouse. Surveyor's office, west to wall.

365. SEWER AND WATER
1929-1930. 1 volume.
Record of engineer's estimate for sewer and water improvements in township sewer and water districts giving name of owner whose property is affected by such improvements, tract, lot number, and location. No index. Handwritten on printed forms. 200 pages. 18 x 12 x 1. County courthouse. Surveyor's office, west wall.

Ledgers and Inventories

366. LEDGER
1913-1932. 6 volumes.
Account of general office expenses and salaries of employees of surveyor's office giving name of person employed and salary each received; also list of improvements on county roads, ditches, bridges, and culverts giving location and cost of project. Alphabetically arranged. Handwritten on printed forms. Condition poor. Volumes average 600 pages. 12 x 8 x 1. County courthouse.
> 1913-1916, 2 volumes. Surveyor's storage, attic.
> 1917-1932, 4 volumes. Surveyor's office, west to wall.

367. TIME BOOK
1913-1932. 9 volumes. (1925, missing).
List of employees in county surveyor's office giving name, hours worked, classification, and salary received. Chronologically arranged. Handwritten on printed forms. Volumes average 600 pages. 15 x 10 x 2. County courthouse.
> 1913-1924, 5 volumes. Surveyor's storage, attic.
> 1926-1932, 4 volumes. Surveyor's office, west to wall.

368. ANNUAL INVENTORY OF COUNTY PROPERTY
1926—. 1 volume.
Record of county owned properties such as machinery, equipment, etc, giving identification, description, valuation of each article. Arranged by county offices. Typed on printed forms. 200 pages. 13 x 11 x 2. County courthouse. Surveyor's office, west wall.

369. ANNUAL INVENTORY OF TOWNSHIP PROPERTY
1926—. 1 volume.
Record of machinery and equipment belonging to various townships giving description, identification, location, and valuation. Alphabetically arranged by names of townships. Handwritten on printed forms. 100 pages. 13 x 11 x 1. County courthouse. Surveyor's office, west wall.

Maps and Plat Books

370. ATLAS AND DIRECTORY OF TRUMBULL COUNTY
1898. 1 volume.
Atlas containing maps and plats of Trumbull County, list of freeholders, individual sketches, and historical data; also photographs and brief biographies of leading citizens. Alphabetically arranged. Printed. Condition poor. 210 pages. 20 x 18 x 1. County courthouse. Surveyor's office, west wall.

371. ATLAS OF MAHONING COUNTY AND TOWNSHIPS OF TRUMBULL ADJOINING
1914. 2 volumes.

Engraved plats of Mahoning County, cities, towns, and villages; also townships in Trumbull County adjoining. No index. Printed. Volumes average 100 pages. 24 x 14 x 2. County courthouse.

    1914, 1 volume. Surveyor's office.

    1914, 1 volume. Surveyor's storage, attic.

372. MAPS OF BROOKFIELD TOWNSHIP SANITARY SEWER DISTRICT
1923. 1 volume.

Maps and prints used for purpose of constructing sewers in Brookfield Township. Prepared by county engineer. Scale, 1 inch equals 50 feet. 130 maps, 22 x 13. County courthouse. Surveyor's office, west wall.

373. MAPS OF HOWLAND AND LIBERTY TOWNSHIP SANITARY SEWERS
1925. 1 volume.

Maps used for purpose of constructing sanitary sewers and Howland and Liberty Townships. Prepared by county engineer. Scale, 1 inch equals 50 feet. Approximately 100 maps, 22 x 13. County courthouse. Surveyor's office, west wall.

374. MAPS AND PLATS
1884-1932. 1 volume.

Individual maps and plats of land surveyed by various county surveyors. Various scales, 250 maps, 16 x 13. County courthouse. Surveyor's office, west wall.

375. MAPS OF TRUMBULL COUNTY
n. d, 100 rolls and bundles.

Maps used for purpose of making improvements in county; original plans for courthouse are included. Prepared by various engineers. Various sizes. County courthouse. Surveyor's office, west wall.

376. MAPS OF TRUMBULL COUNTY ROADS
1917. 1 volume.

Maps showing location, width, and lengths of various county roads. Prepared by county engineers. Scales not shown. 50 maps, 18 x 15. County courthouse. Surveyor's office, west wall.

377. MAPS OF WARREN SANITARY DISTRICT NO. 1
1923. 1 volume.

Maps used for purpose of constructing sanitary sewers in Warren city showing location, elevation, and lengths of each. Prepared by county engineer. Scale, 1 inch equals 50 feet. 68 maps, 22 x 13. County courthouse. Surveyor's office, west wall.

The responsibility for supervising and conducting elections in the county is placed in the hands of the state deputy supervisors of elections or the county board of elections. This board, consisting of four qualified voters in the county, is appointed for a four-year term by the secretary of state, who, by virtue of his office, is the chief election official of the state. On the first Monday in March in the even-numbered years the secretary of state appoints two board members, one of whom is from the political party which cast the highest number of votes in the state for the office of governor at the last preceding state election, and the other from the political party which casts the next highest votes at such election. (G. C. sec. 4,785-8. For the method of appointment when the term of each of the four members of the board expires on the same date see G. C. sec. 4,758-8a). The board members may be removed by the secretary of state for the neglect of duty, malfeasance, misfeasance, or nonfeasance in office; for willful violation of the election laws; or for other good and sufficient causes. (G. C. sec. 7,585-11). The compensation of the members is determined on the basis of population of the county and is paid by the county. (G. C. sec.4,785-18). Similarly the expenses of the county board are paid from the county treasury, "in pursuance of appropriations by the county commissioners," in the same manner as other expenses are paid. (G. C. sec. 4,785-20).

The person so appointed by the secretary, meeting five days after their appointment, select one of their members as chairman, who presides at the meetings; and a resident elector of the county, other than a member of the board, as clerk. (G. C. sec. 4,785-10). The board is vested with authority to establish, define, and provide election precincts; fix places of registration; provide for the purchase, preservation and maintenance of voting booths, ballot boxes, books, maps, flags, blanks, cards of instruction and other equipment used in registration. (G. C. sec. 4,785-13). The board is authorized, further, to issue rules, regulations, and instructions not inconsistent with the law or contrary to the rules and regulations as established by the chief election official. (G. C. sec. 4,785-13).

Besides providing places of voting and equipment, the board is authorized to appoint clerks and other officers of elections. On or before the first day of September before each November election the board by a majority of vote is authorized, after careful examination and investigation as to the qualifications, to appoint for each precinct six "competent persons, four as judges and two as clerks, who shall constitute the election officers of such precinct." Not more than two of the judges and one of the clerks, states the law, "shall be members of the same political party." Precinct election officers, appointed for a one-year term, may be removed by the board for neglect of duty, malfeasance or misconduct in office. (G. C. sec. 4,785-25).

The board is authorized to receive and examine and certify the sufficiency and validity of nominating petitions. They receive the election returns, canvass the returns, make abstracts thereof and transmit them to proper authorities. They issue certificates of elections on forms prescribed by the secretary of state and report annually to the same official, on forms prescribed by him, the number of voters registered, elections held, votes cast, and other information as the secretary of state may require. Moreover, the board prepares and submits to the proper authorities a budget estimating the cost of elections for the ensuing year. (G. C. sec. 4,788-13).

Finally, the board is empowered to investigate irregularities, nonperformance of duty, or violation of election laws by election officials. For the purpose of conducting investigations they may administer oaths, issue subpoenas, summon witnesses, and compel the presentation of books, papers, and records in connection with any investigation and report the facts to the prosecuting attorney. (G. C. sec. 4,785-13).

(The secretary of state, in 1930, ruled that the members of the various boards of elections were to be considered as state officials. This had reference to appointments made under sec. 4,785-8a of the General Code. See *Supplements to Page's Annotated General Code 1926 to 1935,* George C. Trautwein, ed., Cincinnati, 1935, note p. 688).

All records of this office are located in the County Court House, Board of Elections' office, 1st floor.

378. BALLOTS
1936. 136 ballot boxes.
Ballots cast in primary held in May, 1936 showing names of candidates and office sought. These records are usually destroyed in ninety days as permitted by law. Arranged by warrants and precinct. 20 x 12 x 6. East wall.

379. MINUTE BOOK
1891—. 4 volumes.

Record of meetings of board of elections showing names of members present and nature of business acted upon. No index. 1891-1928, handwritten; 1928—, typed. Condition fair. Volumes average 285 pages. 17 x 10 x .75. Northeast wall.

380. POLL BOOKS AND TALLY SHEETS
n. d. 14 file boxes and bundles.
1932—. 153 file boxes.

Alphabetical list of registered voters for the use of precinct workers giving name and address of elector; also signature of elector that voted. The tally sheets give total votes received by each candidate in precinct. Arranged by wards and precincts. 20 x 12 x 12. East and north walls.

381. POLL LIST
n. d. 61 volumes.

Alphabetical list of registered voters in each ward and precinct giving names and addresses of voters. Records change as elector changes place of residence. Alphabetically arranged. Typed on printed forms. Volumes average 50 pages. (loose- leaf) 14 x 12 x 1. East wall.

382. REGISTER OF ABSENT ELECTORS
1918—. 1 volume.

Numerical list of electors who for satisfactory reasons will not be present on day of election to vote. When such an elector is permitted to vote in advance the record gives name of elector, his address, and ward and precinct. Numerically arranged. Handwritten on printed forms. 100 pages. 14 x 8 x 1. North wall.

383. REGISTERED VOTERS
n. d. 510 file boxes.

File register of electors giving their names, addresses, wards, and precincts. Alphabetically arranged by wards and precincts. Kardex system. 4.25 x 8.25. South wall.

The county board of education, a modern administrative and supervisory agency developed during the last two decades, supplanted the smaller educational units, which, established during the earlier period of Ohio history, became inefficient and unable to meet the modern requirements as demanded by rural communities.

During the earlier period of Ohio history educational administration, due to the newness of the state, the sparseness of the population, and undeveloped means of transportation was, by necessity, local in character. For fourteen years after the admission of Ohio as a state, though the constitution stated that means of education should be encouraged by the general assembly, no legislation was enacted for public schools. (*Ohio Const. 1802*, Art. VIII, sec. 3, 25, 17). It was not until 1817 that the legislature authorized six or more people in the township to form associations to build school houses and to be incorporated for educational purposes. (15 O. L. 407). This was a beginning, but as yet the values of an educational system were not readily perceived by those engaged in subduing a stubborn wilderness.

The first permanent law for the organization of schools in Ohio was passed in 1821. Under the provision of this act, the electors of the township were authorized to vote on the proposition of dividing the townships into school districts. If the proposition carried, three school commissioners were to be elected, who, in turn, were authorized to select a clerk and a collector who should act as a treasurer. They were authorized, also, to levy taxes for the support of schools and to hire teachers. (19 O. L. 54).

As education began to advance in the early years of the nineteenth century, some kind of state control was needed. Accordingly, in 1837, the office of state superintendent of schools was established. A year later an act was passed making the county auditor also the county superintendent of schools and, in each township the clerk was made superintendent of the smaller unit. The county superintendent was made responsible to the state superintendent in all educational affairs. In the same year each incorporated city, town or borough, not regulated by a charter was made a separate school district. The voters in each district were authorized to elect three directors. (31 O. L. 21). The effectiveness of this organization, however, was destroyed in 1840, when the legislature abolished the office of state superintendent and the secretary of state took over his functions tabulating and transmitting school statistics. (38 O. L. 130). Seven years later, twenty-five counties were allowed to have county superintendents, and in 1848 the provisions of the previous act were extended to all counties in the state. (46 O. L. 86).

Although marked changes were made in the curriculum of the schools, the history of education in Ohio from 1850 to the early part of the twentieth century was largely one of the gradual transference of powers from districts to townships, and from townships to county in the interest of a better system of education. It was not, however, until within the last three decades that the county became the unit for educational administration. (70 O. L. 195, 204; 97 O. L. 354).

The first permanent law for the establishment of a county board of education, though the county superintendent was known as early as 1838, was enacted in 1914. Under this act the school districts were classified, and provision was made for a county school district, exclusive of the territory embraced in any city or village desiring exemption. The county district was to be under the supervision of five board members elected by the presidents of the village and rural school boards. The members were to hold office for one, two, three, four, and five years respectively, and each year one member was to be selected.

The county board of education was authorized to change school district lines, afford transportation for children living more than two miles from a schoolhouse; appoint a county superintendent; and certify annually to the county auditor the number of teachers and superintendents employed, their salaries, and the amount apportioned for each school district. The county superintendent, acting as secretary of the board, was required to keep a full record of the proceedings of the board properly indexed, in a book provided for that purpose. Each motion, with the person making it and the vote thereon, was to be entered on the record. (104 O. L. 133; 108 O. L. pt. 1, 704).

The county was divided into administrative divisions containing one or more villages or rural school districts. Each district was to be under the supervision of a district superintendent who was required to visit the schools in his charge; direct and assist teachers in the performance of the duties; and classify and control promotions of pupils. Moreover he was required to report annually to the county superintendent on matters under his charge, assemble teachers for the purpose of certifying curricular matters, discipline, and school management. (104 O. L. 133-145).

Significant changes were made by the act of 1920. Under it the county board members became elective. They were authorized to appoint one or more assistant county superintendents for a term of three years. The board was authorized to publish, with the advice and consent of the county superintendent, a minimum course of study to serve as a guide to local school members. The same act abolished the office of district superintendent. (G. C. sec. 4,728-1, 4,729; 108 O. L. pt. 1, 706).

The county organization has placed the rural schools on a plane of equality with the city schools. The consolidation of the smaller units has eliminated the small, ill-equipped schools, and provides under one roof facilities and instructions suited to the needs of the rural children under the supervision of the educational specialist.

All records of the office are located in the office of the County Board of Education, 410 Union Savings and Trust Building, Market Street and Park Avenue, Warren, Ohio.

384. ANNUAL FINANCIAL REPORT, COUNTY SUPERINTENDENT
1922-1936. 4 file boxes, 1 folder.
Compiled financial reports of county superintendent giving detailed settlement of all receipts and expenditures for each school district. Chronologically arranged. 8.5 x 11.

385. ANNUAL STATISTICAL REPORT, COUNTY SUPERINTENDENT
1915-1936. 2 paper folders.
Detailed statistical report of each county school district pertaining to enrollment, attendance, teachers and their training, and transportation information. Chronologically arranged. Folders average 10.25 x 15.5.

386. MINUTE BOOK
1914-1936. 2 volumes.
Record of minutes and proceedings of meetings of county board of education. No index. Typed. Volumes average 200 pages. 15 x 10 x 2.

387. SCHOOL ENUMERATION
1930-1936. 8 file boxes.
School enumeration records for each county school district giving name, age, and address of each child between the age of five and eighteen years. Alphabetically and chronologically arranged. 11 x 12 x 5.

388. COUNTY BOARD OF SCHOOL EXAMINER'S RECORD
1889-1935. 5 volumes. (3, 5-8) (1902, missing).
Record of teachers' certificates showing name and address of teacher, age, examination date, grade, and kind of certificate issued. Alphabetically arranged. Handwritten. Volumes average 300 pages. 15 x 12 x 2.

One of the recent developments in county health administration has been the establishment of the general health district, or county health department. By an act of the legislature in 1919, the townships and municipalities in each county, exclusive of any city having population of 25,000, were to constitute a general health district. Cities having a population of 25,000 or more were to constitute a municipal health district. Municipalities of not less than 10,000 or more than 25,000 which maintain a board of health meeting the qualifications as set by the legislative act, were authorized, after examination by the state health department, to continue operation as a separate health district. (108 O. L. pt. 1, 238). An amendment passed in December 1919, made each city a health district. The townships and villages in each county were combined into a general health district. Provision was also made whereby a city and general health district might combine for administrative purposes. (108 O. L. pt. 2, 1086).

Under the latter act, the provisions for which are still in force, the mayor of each municipality, not constituting a city health district, and the chairman of the trustees of each township were authorized to meet at the seat of justice and organize by selecting a chairman and a secretary. The organization, known as a district advisory council, selects and appoints a district board of health composed of five members, one of whom must be a physician. The members serve without compensation. (*Ibid.,* 1085).

Within thirty days after their appointment the members of the district or "county board of health" organize by selecting one of the members as president and the other member as president *pro-tempore*. The board is authorized to appoint a licensed physician as district health commissioner. This officer, serving as secretary to the board, is designated as state deputy registrar of vital statistics, and is required to report monthly to the state registrar of vital statistics. (G. C. sec. 1,261-32; 108 O. L. pt. 1, 242).

The duties of the county board of health include, among other things, the appointment, upon the recommendation of the health commissioner, of a "wholetime" public health nurse, a clerk, and additional public health nurses, physicians and other persons as may be necessary for the proper conduct of its work. Moreover the board makes a study of the prevalence of disease within the county, communicable diseases, provide for the treatment of venereal diseases, inspection of public charitable, benevolent, correctional, and penal institutions. In addition to this, the board may provide inspection of dairies, stores, restaurants, hotels, and other places where food is manufactured, handled, stored, sold or offered for sale. (108 O. L. pt. 2, 1088-1089). The board is authorized to make any and all regulations it deems necessary for the prevention or restriction of diseases, and the prevention, abolition or suppression of a nuisance. (108 O. L. pt. 2, 1089). The county prosecutor represents the board in legal matters. (which see).

The board may provide for carrying on such laboratory work as may be necessary for the conduct of its work. It may establish a laboratory or contract with existing laboratories for the work. All state institutions, supplied in whole or in part by public funds, most furnish such laboratory service to a county board of health under the terms agreed upon. (108 O. L. pt. 2, 1089).

The work of the health department is financed by public taxation. The board annually estimates, in itemized form, the amount needed for the next fiscal year. Such estimates, certified by the county auditor, are submitted to the county budget commissioners which may reduce any item in such an estimate, but cannot increase any item or the aggregate of all new items. The aggregate amount, as fixed by the budget commissioners, is apportioned by the county health district on the basis of taxable valuations in such townships and municipalities. (*Ibid.,* 1091).

All the records are located in the County Board of Health office, 508 Union Savings and Trust Building, Market Street and Park Avenue, Warren, Ohio.

389. BIRTH RECORD
1922—. 2 volumes.
Birth record giving sex, color, year, month, and date of birth, mother's maiden name, and whether legitimate or illegitimate. Alphabetically arranged. Handwritten on printed forms. Volumes average 200 pages. (loose-leaf) 14 x 12 x 2.

390. DEATH RECORD
1922—. 2 volumes.
Record giving day, month, and year of death; also sex, color, and cause of death. Alphabetically arranged. Handwritten on printed forms. Volumes average 200 pages. (loose-leaf) 14 x 12 x 2.

391. RECORD OF DISEASES
1922—. 2 volumes.
Record of all diseases reported to county board of health giving nature, etc. Alphabetically arranged. Handwritten on printed forms. Condition fair. Volumes average 200 pages. (loose-leaf) 24 x 8 x 2.

Old age pensions, although well-known in Europe at the end of the nineteenth and beginning of the twentieth century and in a few American states during the same period, were not provided for in Ohio until recently. (Arthur Lyon Cross, *A Short History of England and Greater Britain,* N. Y., 1925, 746-747; J Salwin Schapiro, *Modern and Contemporary European History 1815-1925,* N. Y., 1923, 295). During the depression years the sigh of thousands of aged persons who had lost their homes and savings, and, as a result of such losses faced starvation, touched the sensibilities of Ohioans. Accordingly, in 1933, an "Old Age Pension" law, proposed by initiative petition, was voted upon at the general election of that year providing for the granting of aid to the aged in Ohio under certain conditions. The law was adopted by a majority of electors voting thereon. (115 O. L. pt. 2, 431-439). The act, as amended in 1936, provides, among other things, that any person sixty-five years of age or upwards (excluding persons confined in any penal or corrective institution or the state hospital) who is a citizen of the United States, who has resided in Ohio for not less than five years during the nine prior to making application for aid, and, who has resided in the county, wherein application for aid is made, for one year, is eligible to receive a pension, providing his income from all and every source does not exceed $360 per year. (116 O. L. pt. 2, 1st s. sess. H. 605; 116 O. L. pt. 2, s, sess. H. 558). Moreover the applicant must be unable to support himself, and have no husband, wife, child or other person who is legally responsible for his support. (115 O. L. pt. 2, 431-439). In addition to this, the net value of all real and personal property of the applicant, if single, less all encumbrance and liens, does not exceed $3,000; or if married the net value of the property of husband and wife shall not exceed $4,000. (115 O. L. pt. 2, 431-439). It may be required that such property, as a condition precedent to payment of aid, be transferred to the division of aid for the aged in trust. This provision does not, however, prohibit the applicant or his wife from occupying such property during their lifetime.

For the purpose of ministering the old age pension law there was created in the department of public welfare a division of aid for the aged. The chief of the division of aid for the aged, appointed by the director of public welfare with the approval of the governor, is authorized to appoint all necessary assistants, clerks, stenographers, and other employees and fix their salaries, subject to approval of the director of public welfare. (115 O. L. pt. 2, 431-439).

In each county the commissioners constitute a board for administering the act. However, if the commissioners, by a majority vote, decline to serve in such a capacity, the state director is authorized, with the consent of the director of public welfare, to appoint a board consisting of three or five members, who, like the commissioners, serve without compensation. The local boards are required to keep such reports as the division may prescribe, and are also authorized to employ, subject to the approval of the division, such investigators, clerks, and other employees as are necessary for the performance of its duties. (*Ibid.,* pt. 2. 431-439).

Applications for relief are made annually to the local board. Each applicant is thoroughly investigated. In its investigations the local board is not bound by common law or statutory rules of evidence, but is authorized to make investigations in such a manner as seems "best calculated to conform to substantial justice." For the purpose of its investigations, each county board has the power to compel the attendance and testimony of witnesses. Decisions of the local boards may be appealed to the division. (115 O. L. pt. 2, 431-439).

After the applicants have been investigated by the local board, "certificates of aid" are granted to persons entitled to relieve in conformity with the provisions of the law. Each certificate containing the applicant's name and the pension allowed, as well as the records pertaining to the investigation, is forwarded to the division. The division may approve, modify, or reject the certificate and findings of the board. (115 O. L. Pt. 2, 435).

Under the provisions of this act the state becomes the general guardian of public and private welfare. The pension system relief the over-increasing burden placed upon county infirmaries, which, under the most favorable conditions, are a poor substitute for homes. Although $2,625,000 was appropriated by the legislature for old age pensions in the early part of 1935, the cost to the public in the long run, should not be much greater than the antiquated system of support in charitable institutions. (116 O. L. 510).

392. COUNTY BOARD OF AID FOR THE AGED
1934. 1 volume.

Minutes and records of board of commissioners pertaining to old age pensions. Alphabetically arranged. Typed. 180 pages. 20 x 14 x 1. County courthouse, County Commissioners Office, 2nd floor, northeast wall.

393. TRUMBULL COUNTY RELIEF COMMISSION

1933—. 2 volumes.

Minutes and records of county relief commission. No index. Typed. Volumes average 340 pages. 20 x 14 x 1.75. County courthouse, County Commissioners Office, 2nd floor, northeast wall.

All locations are Warren, Ohio, unless otherwise noted.

Auditor
https://www.co.trumbull.oh.us/Auditor
161 High Street NW

Clerk of Courts
https://www.co.trumbull.oh.us/Clerk
161 High Street NW

Coroner
http://coroner.co.trumbull.oh.us/
2931-B Youngstown Road, SE

County Commissioners
https://www.co.trumbull.oh.us/commissioners
160 High Street NW

Court of Appeals
https://www.co.trumbull.oh.us/11thcourt/
11 High Street, NE

Court of Common Pleas
http://commonpleas.co.trumbull.oh.us/
161 High Street NW

Dog Warden
http://dogwarden.co.trumbull.oh.us/
7501 Anderson Avenue

Educational Service Center
https://www.trumbullesc.org/
6000 Youngstown Warren Road
Niles, OH 44446

Election Board
https://boe.co.trumbull.oh.gov/
2947 Youngstown Rd. SE

Engineer
https://www.co.trumbull.oh.us/engineer/
650 North River Road NW

Fair
https://trumbullcountyfair.com/
899 Everett Hull Road
Cortland, OH 44410

Health Department
http://www.tcchd.org/
194 W. Main Street
Cortland, OH 44410

Probate Court
https://www.trumbullprobate.org/
161 High Street NW

Prosecutor
https://www.co.trumbull.oh.us/prosecutor/
160 High Street NW

Recorder
https://www.co.trumbull.oh.us/recorder/
60 High Street NW

Sanitary Engineer
https://www.co.trumbull.oh.us/Sanitary-Engineer/
842 Youngstown-Kingsville Road
Vienna, Ohio 44473-9737

Sheriff
https://www.co.trumbull.oh.us/sheriff/
150 High Street NW

Treasurer
http://treasurer.co.trumbull.oh.us/
County Administration Building, 2nd Floor
160 High Street, NW
FL 2A

Veterans Service
https://trumbullcountyvets.org/
253 E. Market Street

Main non-governmental

FamilySearch
https://www.familysearch.org/search/catalog
  FamilySearch is a free website with digitized records. Records located for Trumbull County include: Auditor, Common Pleas, Justice Court, Probate Court, Recorder's Office, Supreme Court, as well as Recorder, Mahoning County, Ohio, and Recorder, Columbiana County, Ohio. Each of these listings have many items included, such as naturalization, marriages, etc.

Western Reserve Historical Society
10825 East Boulevard
Cleveland, OH
https://www.wrhs.org/
  Western Reserve Historical Society, a part of the Cleveland History Center, has a large collection of information regarding Trumbull County. Searching the library collections with the keyword Trumbull County gives the extensive listing for the county. Please check the website for days of operation.

Warren-Trumbull County Public Library
444 Mahoning Avenue NW
https://wtcpl.org/
  The Local History and Genealogy Center is located at the main library in Warren. Material available include digitized resources, helpful websites, local information and organizations, online research resources, Trumbull Memory Project, and Obituary index search. Some of these items were transcribed from volunteer-generated card files in 2012.

Heritage Books by Jana Sloan Broglin:

*Additions and Corrections to the W.P.A. Inventory
of Adams County, Ohio: West Union*

*Additions and Corrections to the W.P.A. Inventory
of Allen County, Ohio: Lima*

*Additions and Corrections to the W.P.A. Inventory
of Ashland County, Ohio: Ashland*

*Additions and Corrections to the W.P.A. Inventory
of Athens County, Ohio: Athens*

*Additions and Corrections to the W.P.A. Inventory
of Belmont County, Ohio: St. Clairsville*

*Additions and Corrections to the W.P.A. Inventory
of Cuyahoga County, Ohio: Cleveland*

*Additions and Corrections to the W.P.A. Inventory
of Fulton County, Ohio: Wauseon*

*Additions and Corrections to the W.P.A. Inventory
of Geauga County, Ohio: Chardon*

*Additions and Corrections to the W.P.A. Inventory
of Hancock County, Ohio: Findlay*

*Additions and Corrections to the W.P.A. Inventory
of Lake County, Ohio: Painesville*

*Additions and Corrections to the W.P.A. Inventory
of Lorain County, Ohio: Elyria*

*Additions and Corrections to the W.P.A. Inventory
of Lucas County, Ohio: Toledo*

*Additions and Corrections to the W.P.A. Inventory
of Medina County, Ohio: Medina*

*Additions and Corrections to the W.P.A. Inventory
of Muskingum County, Ohio: Zanesville*

*Additions and Corrections to the W.P.A. Inventory
of Seneca County, Ohio: Tiffin*

*Additions and Corrections to the W.P.A. Inventory
of Trumbull County, Ohio: Warren*

*Additions and Corrections to the W.P.A. Inventory
of Wayne County, Ohio: Wooster*

Hookers, Crooks and Kooks, Part I: Hookers

Hookers, Crooks and Kooks, Part II: Crooks and Kooks

Lucas County, Ohio, Index to Deaths, 1867–1908

*Mason County, Kentucky Wills and Estates, 1791–1832,
Second Edition*

www.ingramcontent.com/pod-product-compliance
Lightning Source LLC
Chambersburg PA
CBHW070917270326
41927CB00011B/2612